1/83
Farewell,
Les!

H

Within each of us
    there are
        "moments of truth,"
            times of decision,
                crossroads
        which affect the
            directions of our lives . . .
Farewells are only beginnings . . .

Farewells Are Only Beginnings

ABOUT THE AUTHOR

The poetry of George Betts is poetry of growth and awareness which awakens an understanding of our deepest feelings. His previous books include the best-selling VISIONS OF YOU, MY GIFT TO YOU, and TEARS AND PEBBLES IN MY POCKETS. He is also the co-author of GROWING TOGETHER.

Working with thousands of people in the field of personal growth and self-expression, Dr. Betts and his wife Donni, author of A SHARED JOURNEY: THE BIRTH OF A CHILD and co-author of GROWING TOGETHER, are currently offering self-expression writing workshops, personal growth seminars, and couples and family enhancement weekends. For further information contact Dr. George Betts, c/o Celestial Arts, 231 Adrian Road, Millbrae, California 94030.

Farewells Are Only Beginnings

George Betts

Celestial Arts
Millbrae, California

Photographs by Maria Demarest

Cover and interior design by Betsy Bruno

Copyright © 1977 by George Betts
Celestial Arts, 231 Adrian Road, Millbrae, California 94030

No part of this book may be reproduced by any mechanical, photographic, or electronic process, or in the form of a phonographic recording, nor may it be stored in a retrieval system, transmitted, or otherwise copied for public or private use without the written permission of the publisher.

First printing: November 1977
Manufactured in the United States of America

Library of Congress Cataloging in Publication Data

Betts, George
    Farewells are only beginnings.

    I. Title.
PS3552.E85F3   811'.5'4   77-79887
ISBN 0-89087-211-2
    4 5 6 7 8 — 82 81 80

for Donni,
　Kristi,
　　Ron,
　　　Nancy and Tom

Whoever we are
we hold in our hearts
the memories
of the times
we have lived and loved.

Today is more meaningful
for it is built on
who we were,
where we have been
and the paths
we have traveled . . .

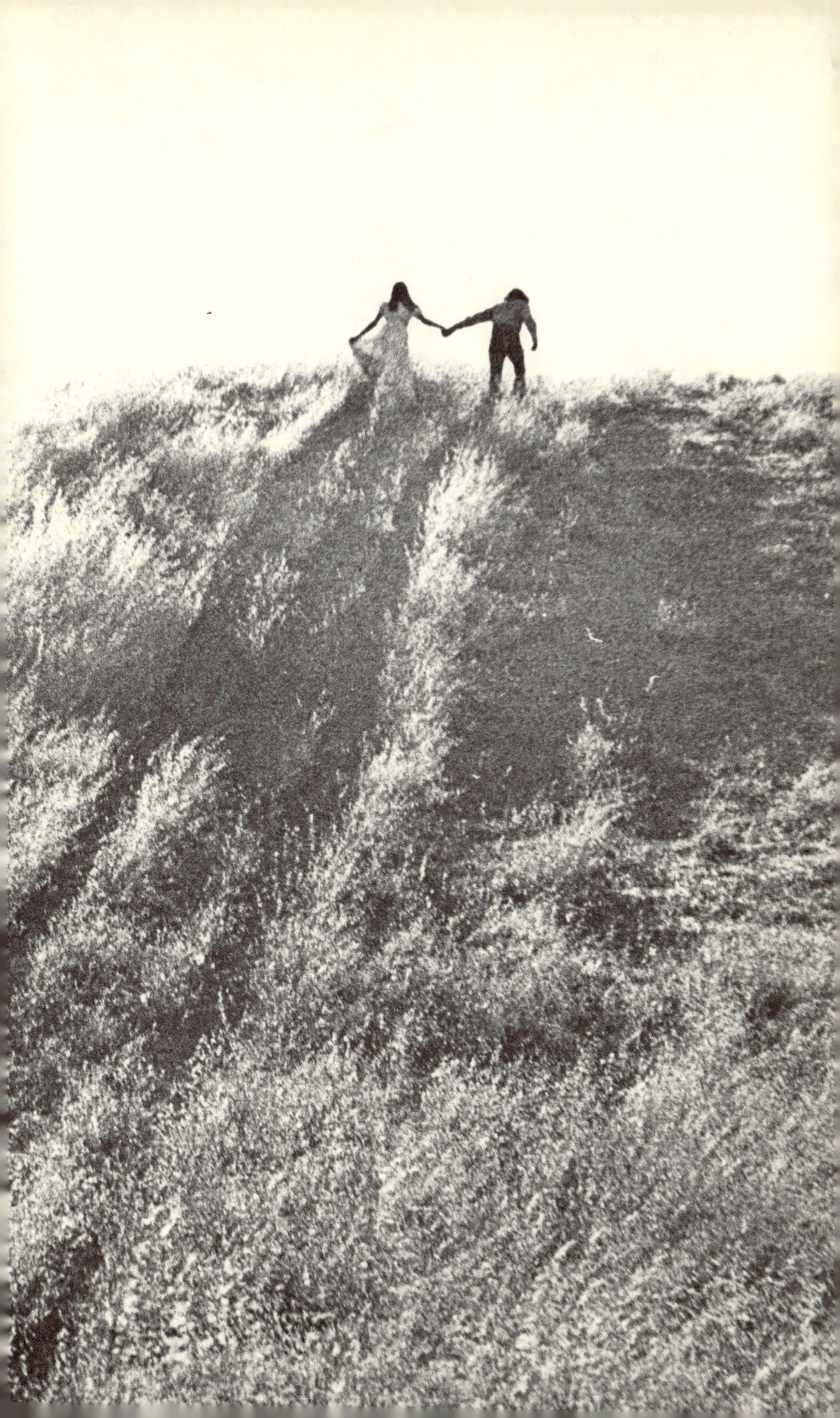

I'm a traveler.
Each mile is a chapter
        of my life.
I seek to turn the pages,
to read between the lines,
    to understand
        the meaning
life is gaining for me.

Today is almost over.
The sun is slowly
        drifting away
but I'll be secure tonight.
I've lived another day.

The pages are being filled
    day by day
        and through my travels
my life is
    becoming more complete.

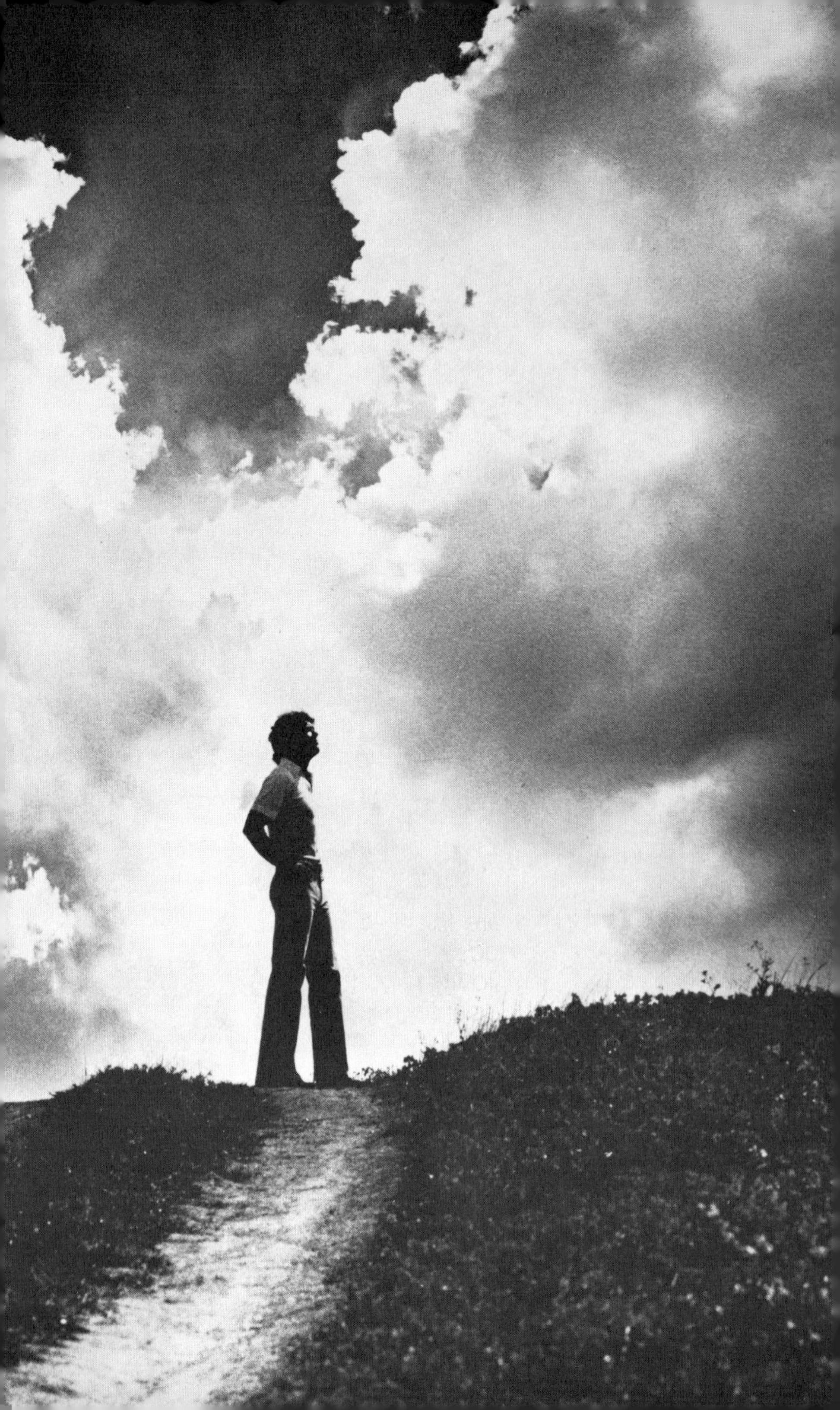

The storm is over,
the clouds are slowly
        drifting away
and the sky is
        becoming blue
           once again.
And slowly,
        from underneath it all
I'm beginning to emerge.
My pace is slowing down,
my face feels more relaxed
and people notice
        that I am changing.

Why do I allow it
        to happen?
Will I learn more this time
or will the clouds
        slowly find me once again
as my journey continues?

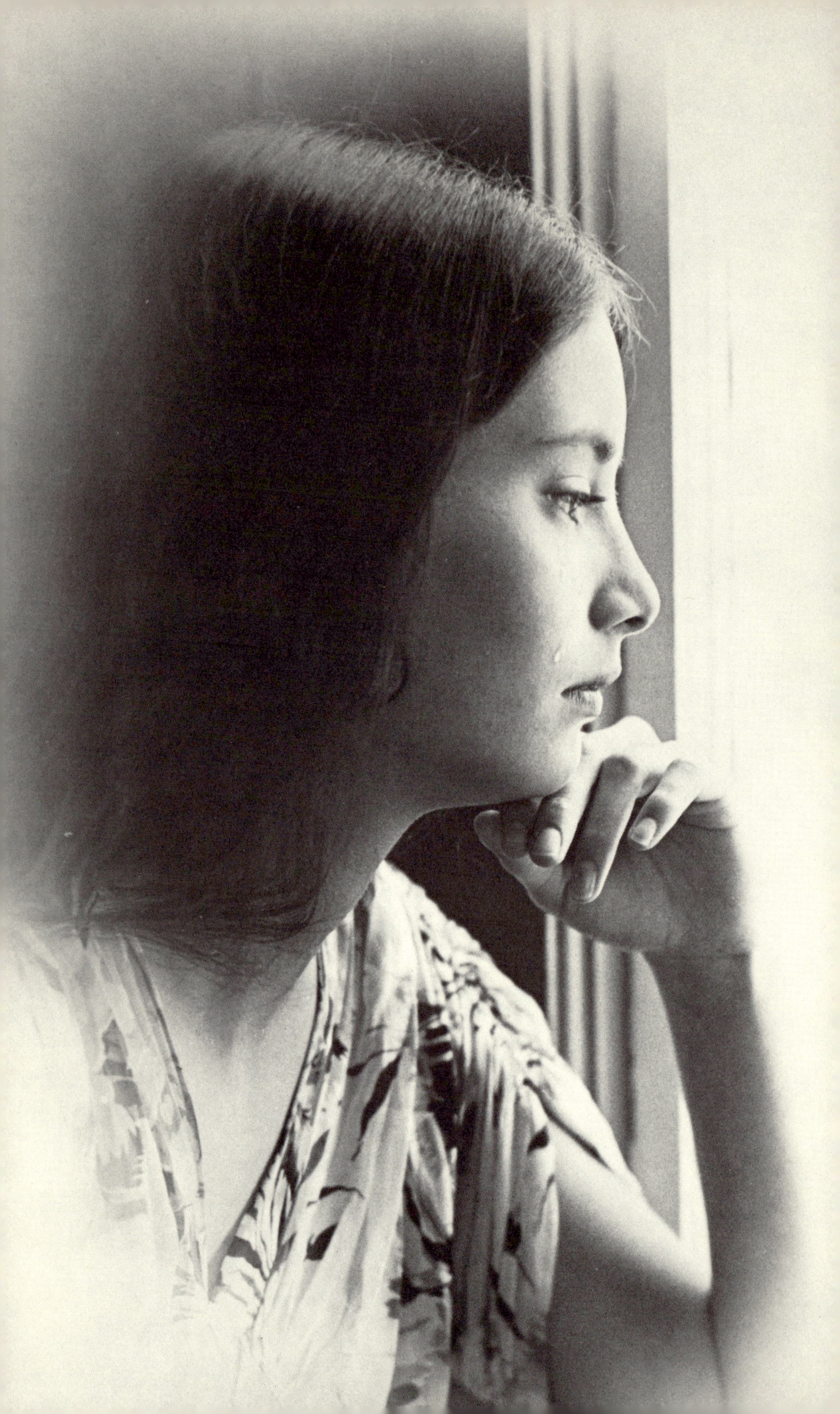

She hurts you
and you hold it inside . . .
never telling her how you feel.

You hurt her
and she holds it inside . . .

Someday
         the dam will break.
I hope you are both strong enough
to endure what you have created.

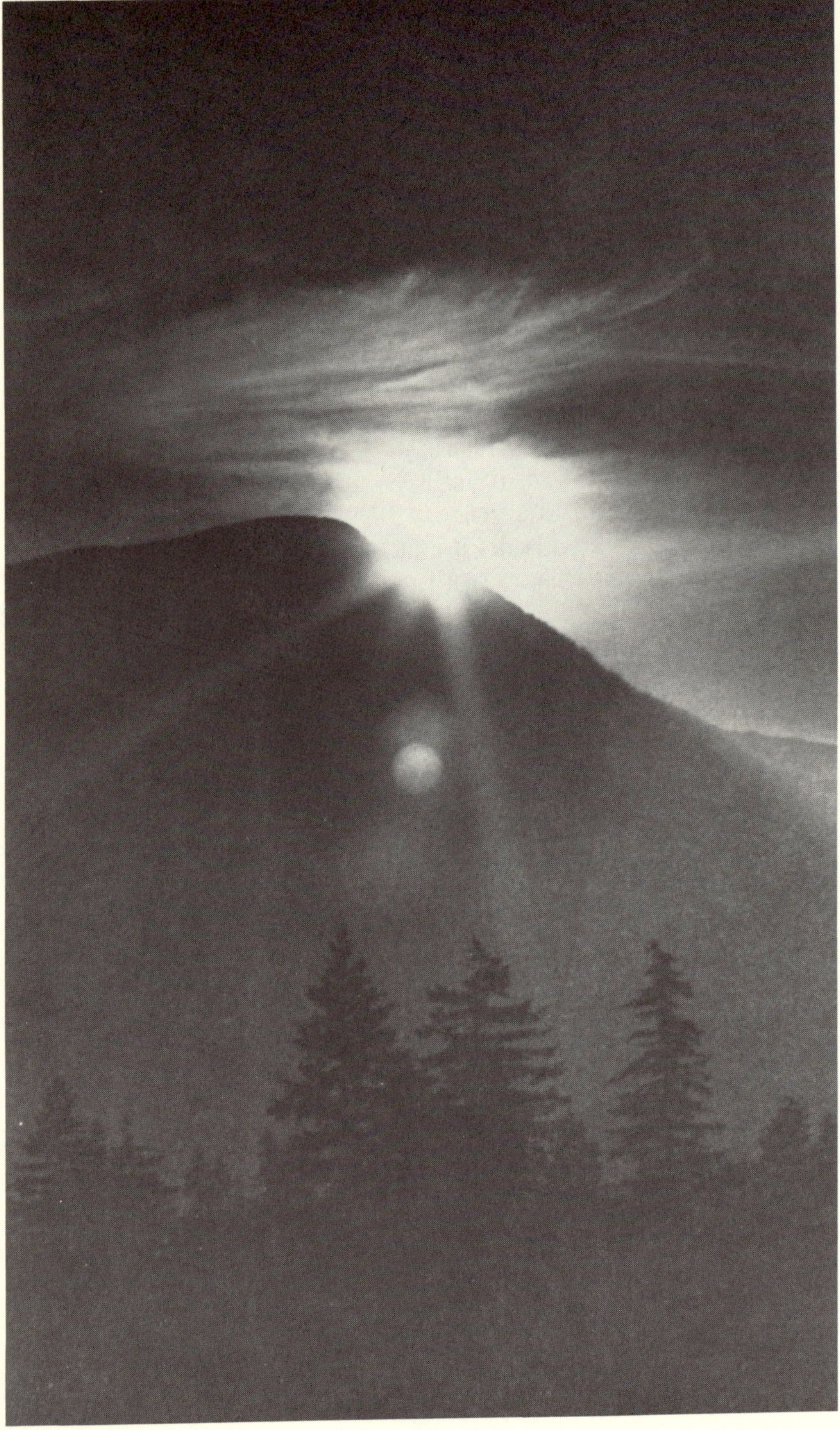

It's late,
long after midnight
and I find myself wide awake,
somewhat relaxed,
but somewhat anxious.

I have so much
but I want more.
Why?
Do I appreciate what I have
or will I only appreciate
what I have when it's too late,
when things have changed?

I'm not sure about me
right now . . .
What is it
that I need?

Get up . . .
        shower
                shave
dress, eat quickly,
            run for the car
                      and my day
begins once again
                at a fast and furious pace.

Today I awoke an hour early
and I had time
        for me
                to enjoy,
to slowly allow
        the day
                to unfold.

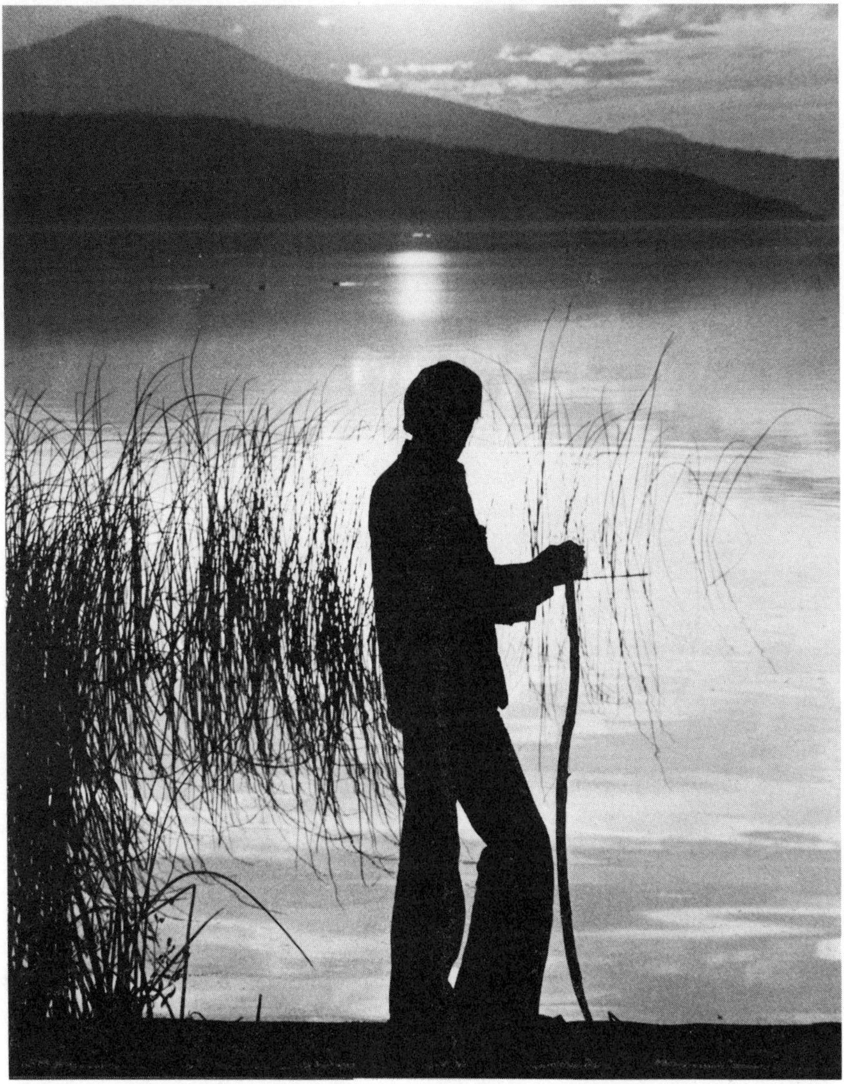

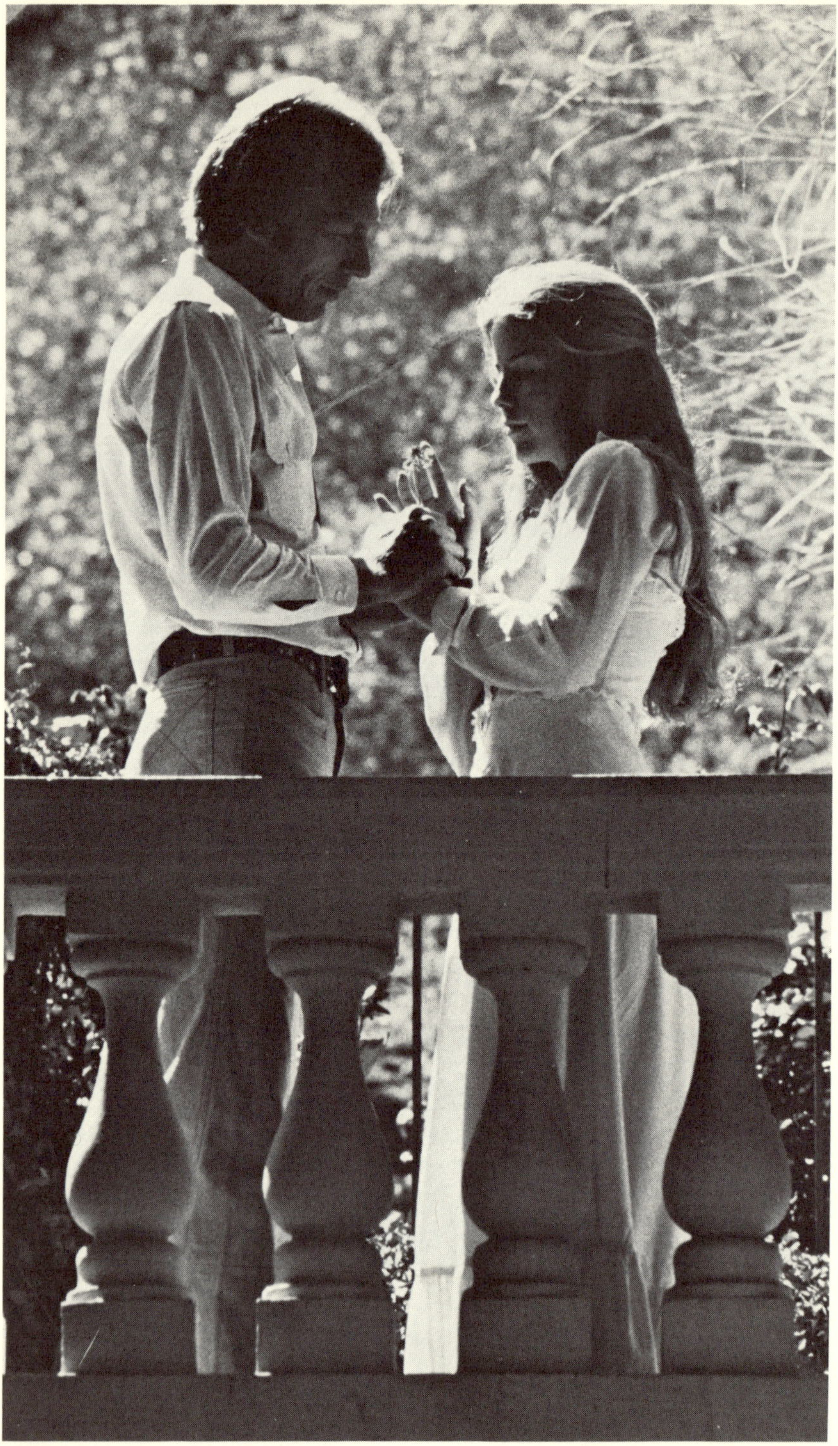

What more can I say?
You trusted me,
    giving me your deepest
        feelings and emotions.
You took a risk . . .
And slowly the conflicts
    were resolved.
The water became calmer,
    the sun appeared,
and I found myself
    filled with emotion . . .
You had trusted me
    with your "self,"
the most essential part of your life.

What more can I say?
I hope I was gentle . . .

Thank you
for loving me enough
      to accept me when I'm hurting
         down
            or angry.
This is a period of crisis
      for me,
a time when I need to pull myself
         together
and because of this
my energy is limited.
I am not able to give enough
         to you.
You patiently love
      and support me,
using your acceptance
         and understanding
    to comfort and nurture me.
You are a strong lady,
patiently standing by my side,
      knowing that tomorrow
         can be a brighter day
and that, once again,
I will have the energy
      and desire to love you
in my own special way.
Because of you I see hope . . .
an opportunity to go beyond today . . .

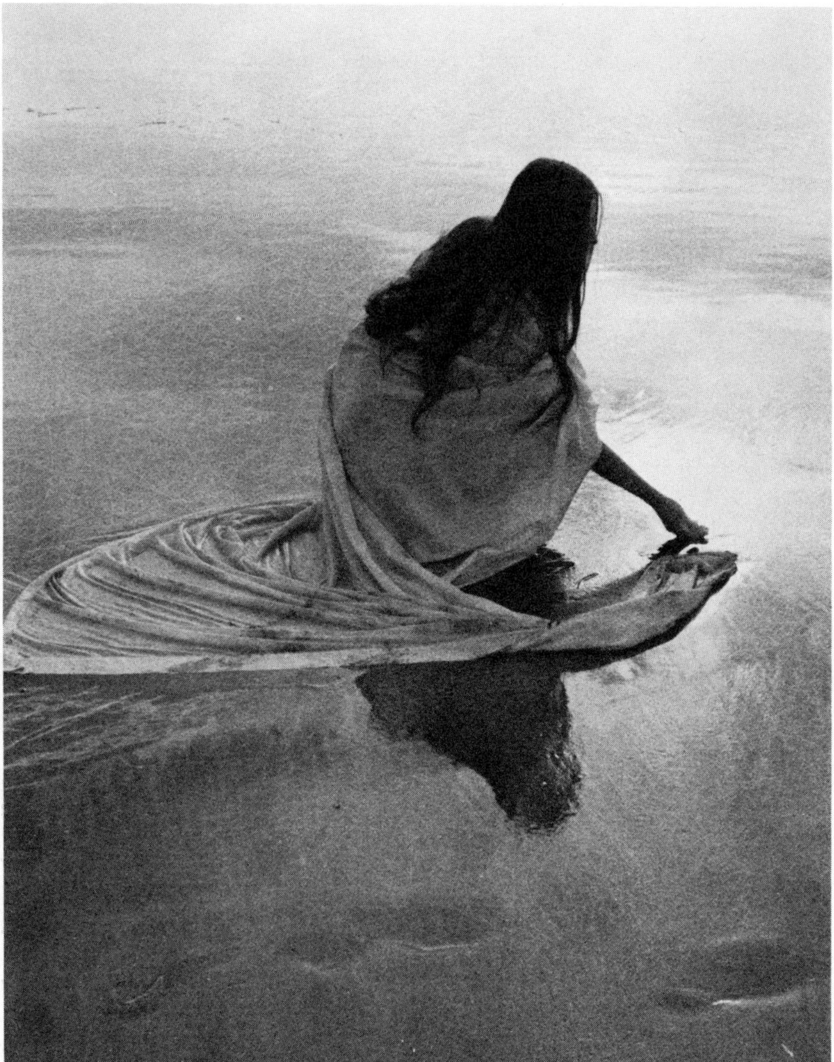

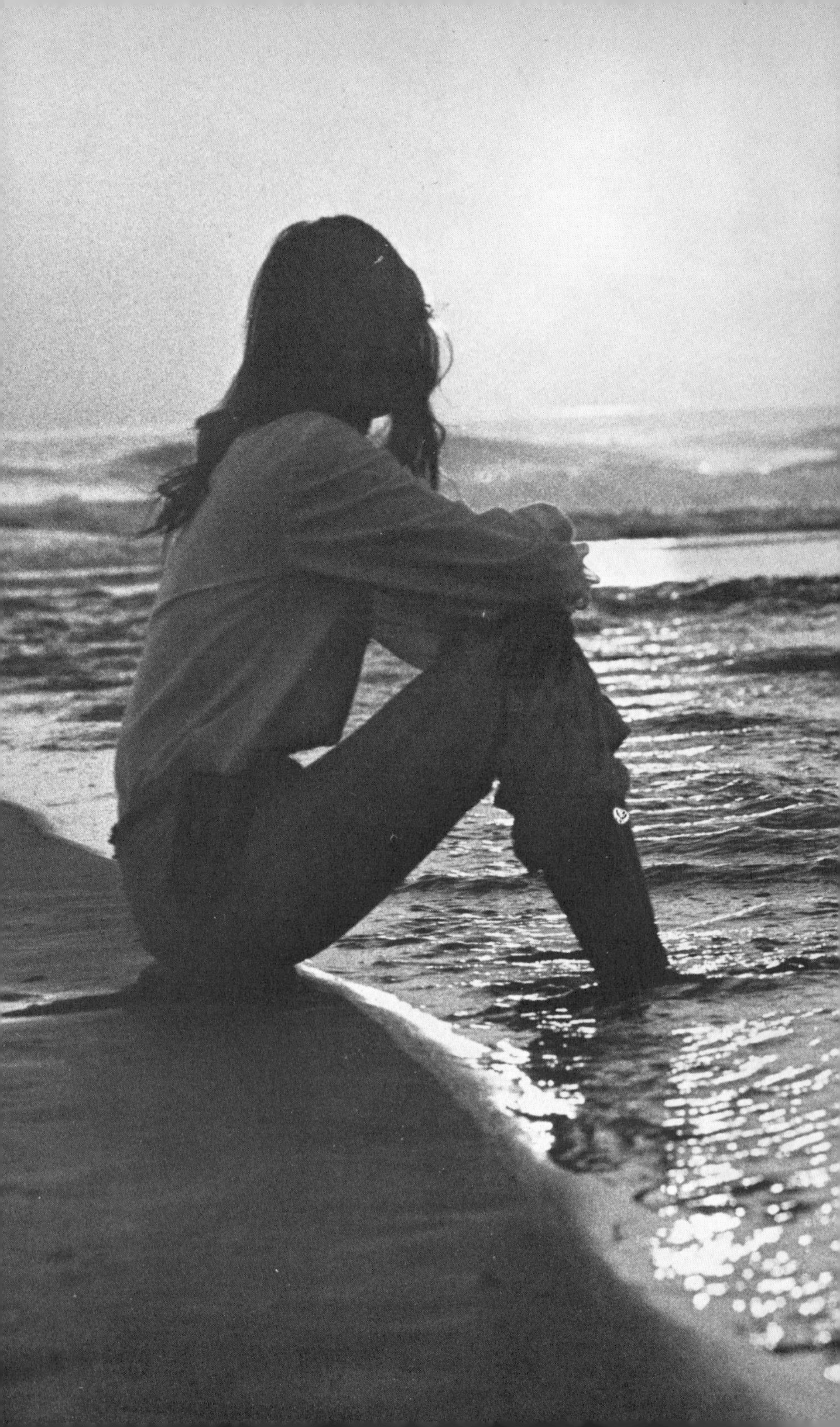

I'm waiting for your return,
not knowing what to expect.

We parted through
          the gates of love,
many years ago,
              but since then we have both
       been bombarded by friends
              and acquaintances,
    responsibilities and
             opportunities.
I remember you
      as you were,
but that was many years ago.
The world is forever changing . . .

I have so many questions
but I remain silent
       in the darkness.
I'm protected, though.
      You can't see my face,
but inside I know
     that you, too,
are hiding, alone,
    in the darkness.

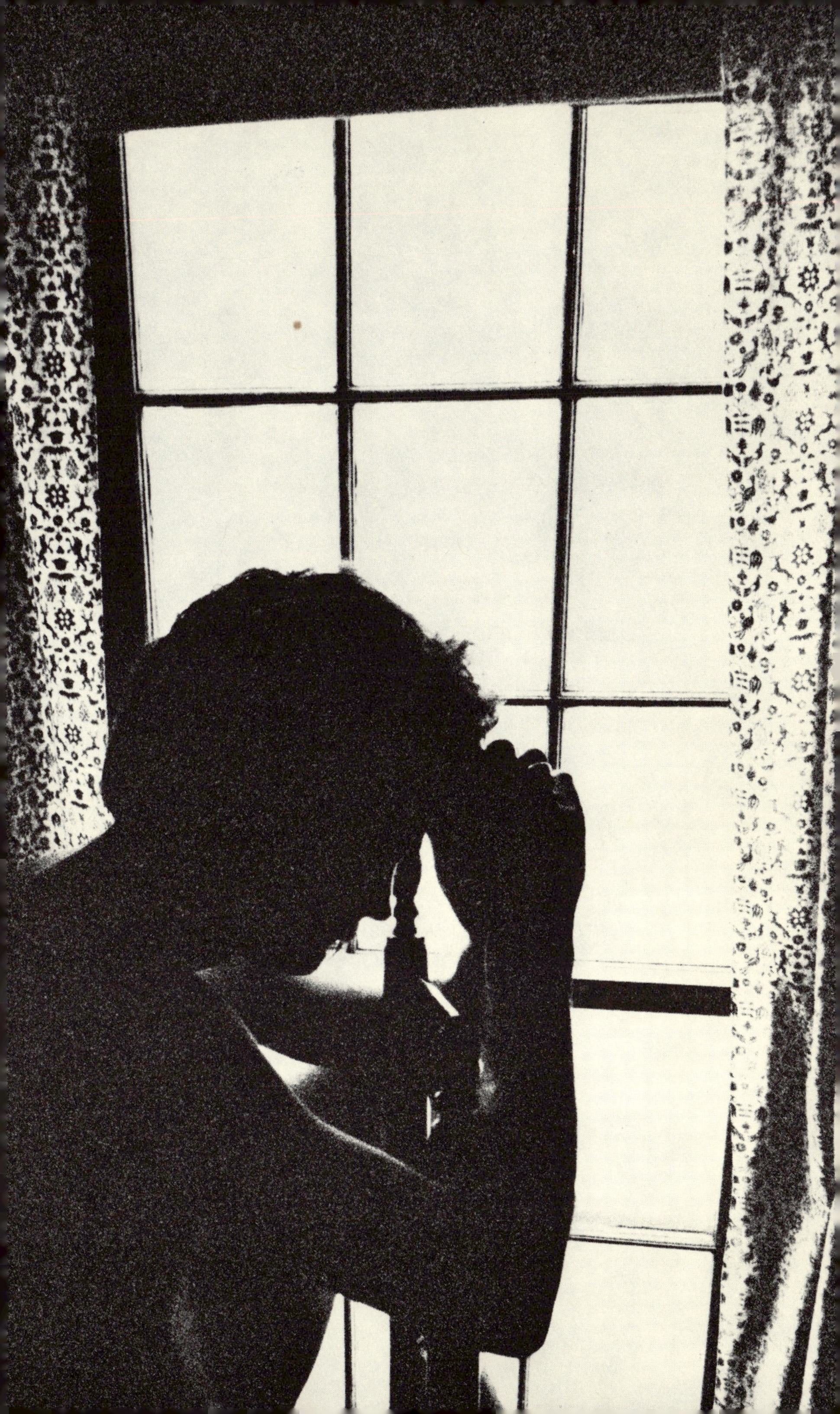

I looked into her eyes . . .
the same eyes
    that were once magical,
       alive, exciting,
          a fountain of life.

And as I gazed,
    searching for a glimpse
       of her past,
I found nothing
    but emptiness,
        sorrow . . .
And without words
    I reached out,
       held her,
for I knew she needed
something that words
       could not express . . .

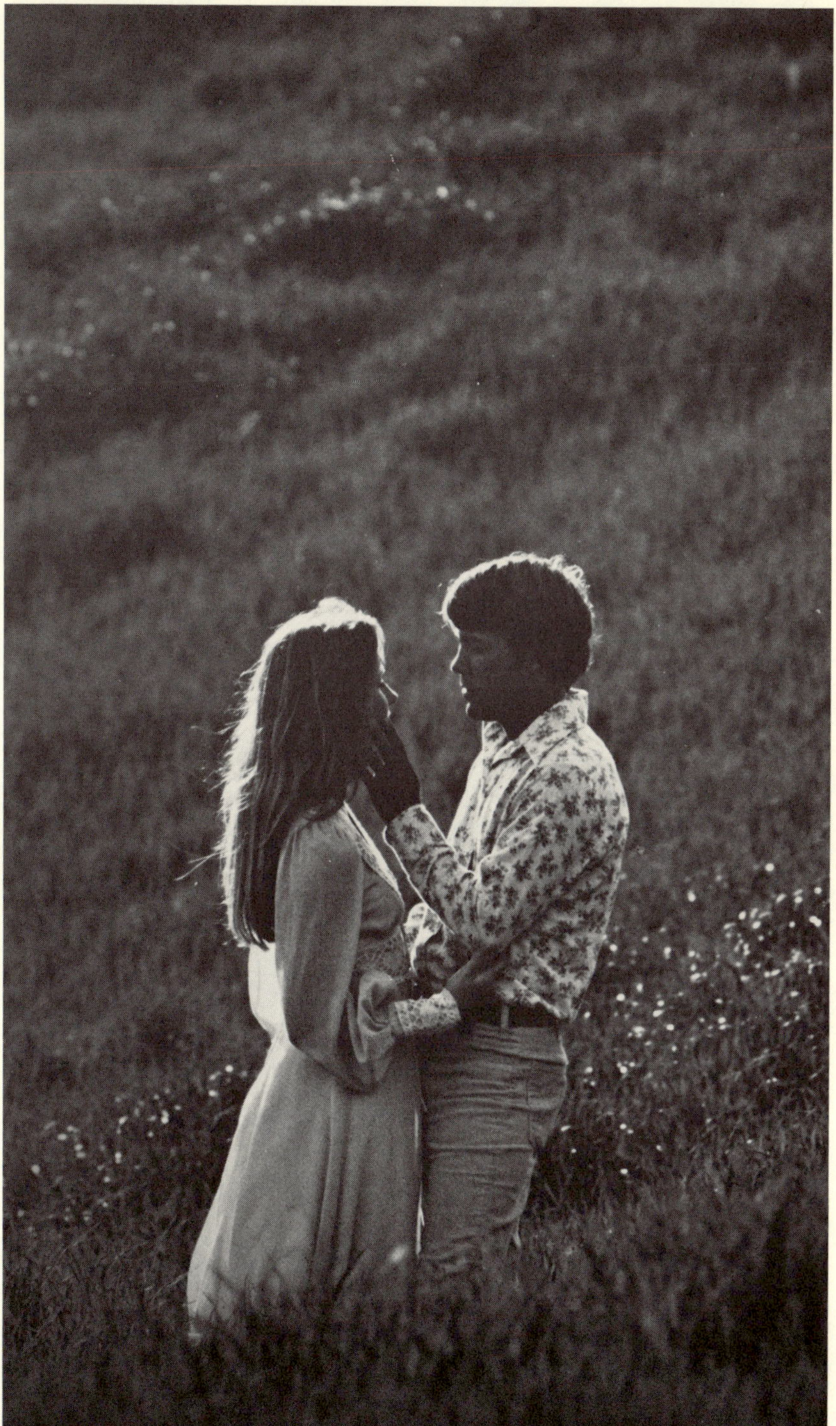

With just a passing thought
you entered my mind
and I knew I needed
    to talk to you tonight,
        to know how you are.

Our phone conversation was clumsy
as we searched for words
but finally you shared
your illness with me,
    telling me of the reports
        and the results.

You spoke with sadness,
    with hesitation, but also
with relief, for you finally
    knew the truth.

As we said goodbye
I searched for words
but found only silence.
All I could say is that
I love you, I'm sorry . . .
    and somewhat afraid . . .

Now,
        hours later,
unable to sleep,
        I find myself
writing,
        expressing my feelings.

You are young and beautiful,
a flower in spring,
beginning to grow and blossom,
but then it hit
        and you found yourself
ill,
afraid of what could be wrong.
I cry for you silently
        and pray for your health.

My eyes close gently,
        your vision appears before me
                and I relive our memories,
                      our times of love,
                our walk in the forest,
and I see you so vividly . . .

I have captured you
        forever
                in my mind . . .
You will always be
        young and beautiful.

Once again I return to the ocean,
and I find it as it always is,
                changing, flowing.
And through the passing days,
                months and years
I have learned
                to ride the waves,
        to accept and love myself,
and to reach out, through risks,
                to others.
As I sit here, absorbed by your beauty,
            I feel your tremendous strength
                    and energy . . .
The sun will soon leave,
                and so will I, refreshed . . .

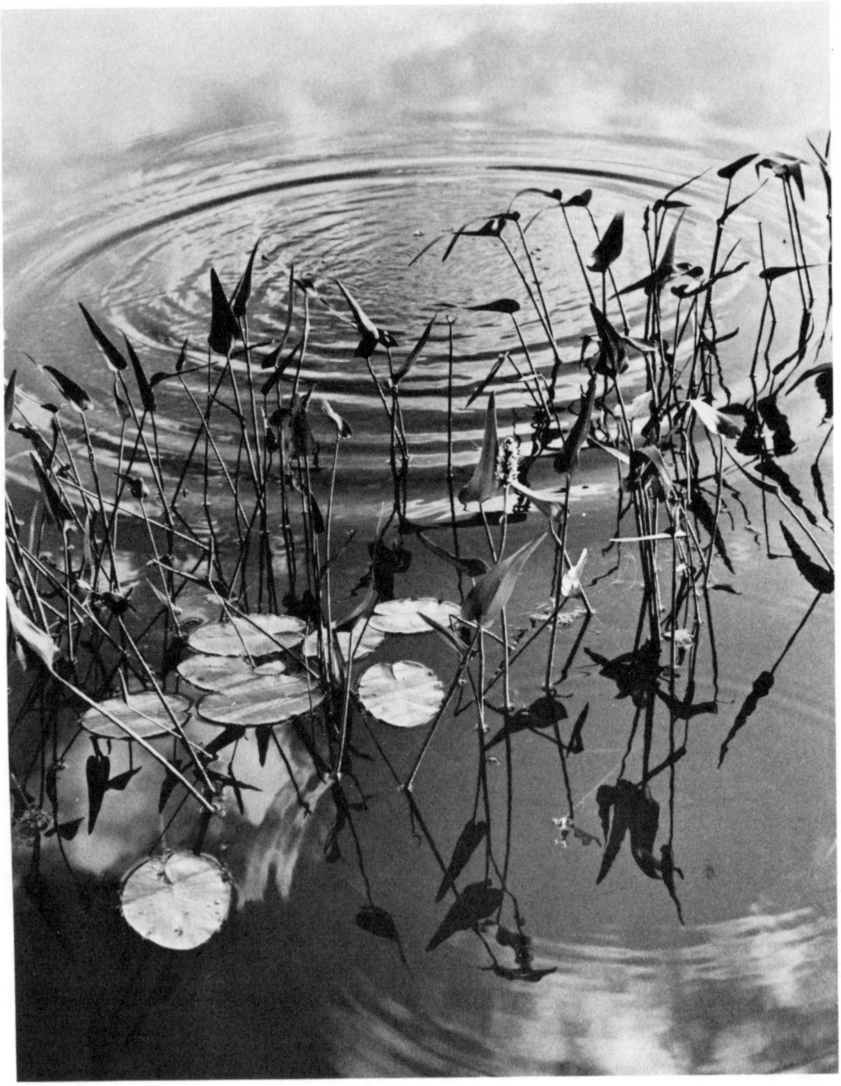

Now I understand.
Most of the time
I spend my energy
dealing with life
but then it happens.
All the pieces fall together
and the puzzle becomes complete.

I value times like now,
going beyond myself,
               my understanding.

Some people have the ability
to create excitement in their lives.
They are the ones who strive,
　　　　　　who grow,
　　　　who give and share.
They are the ones
　　　　　who love . . .

They possess passion . . .
for themselves,
        others,
            nature and experiences.

They have the ability
to see beyond today,
to rise above
        the hectic pace,
to strive for their own perfection . . .

And they are gentle,
for they love themselves
        and they love others . . .

Through their living
        they create peace
                and contentment,
            and at the same time
they create excitement,
for there is always another mountain,
a deeper joy,
        a new dawn . . .

I learned something tonight,
something extremely important.
    I cannot always be the one
        who is best,
            first chosen
    or most popular.
I felt bad because
        I didn't receive
as much attention
        as I wanted
        or needed.
A small amount of insecurity
        crept out.
How to learn from this experience?
I need to reflect . . .
        to sit down and evaluate,
    to realize that I cannot
        be one hundred percent successful,
and that at times
        I will be insecure,
that it's okay to feel like this.

Once again I have relearned
    what it's like to be human . . .
and vulnerable.

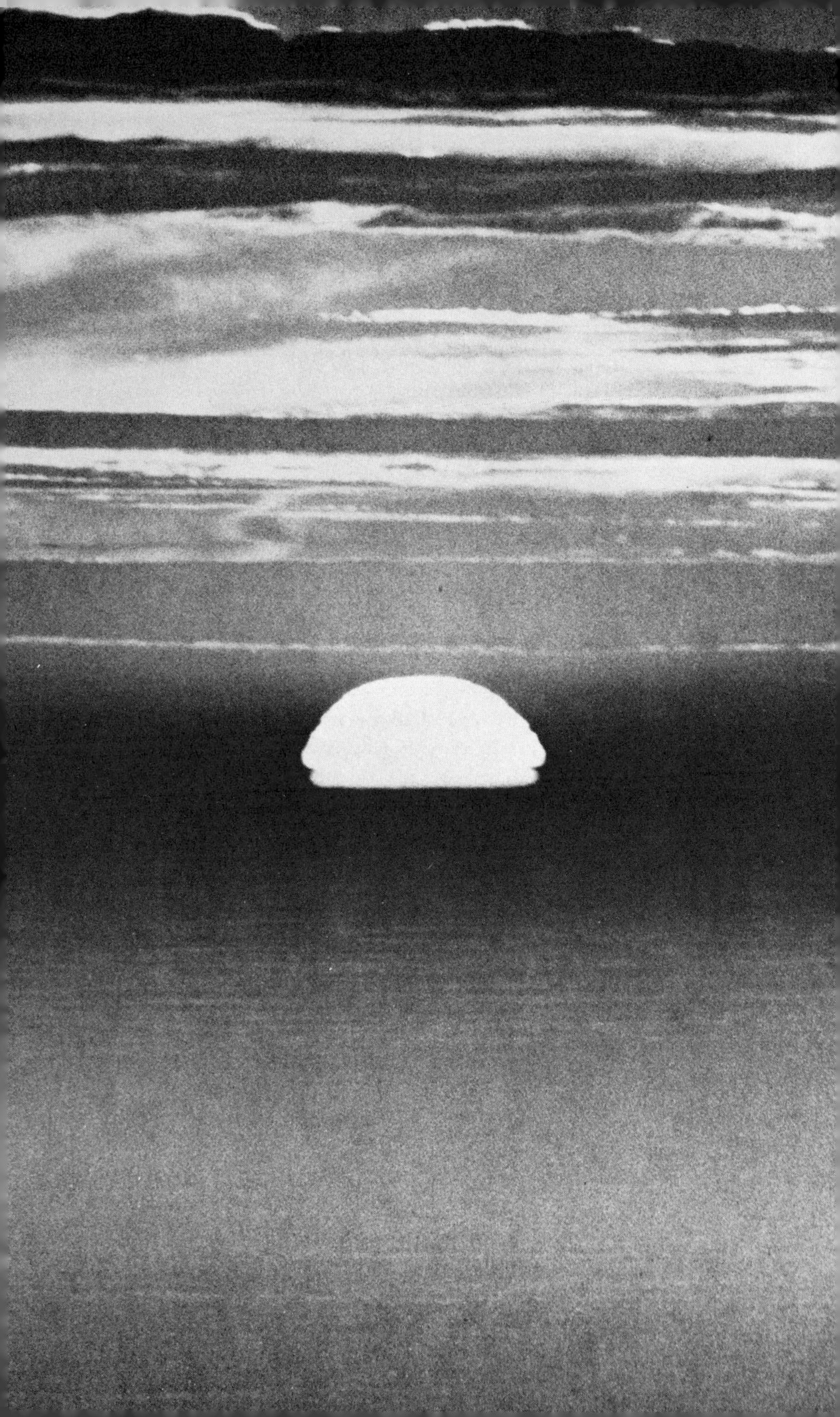

It snowed all day.
We decided not to go out
    and tonight is ours . . .
Just us
    and our new home.
I'm changing,
    rearranging . . .
I no longer seek
    constant motion
with people,
    places
and experiences.
A new dimension
    is being added . . .
    the security and solitude
of our home,
    where we have
a place for everything,
time to settle in,
    and the excitement
    of developing something new,
something that we haven't had
    in the past . . .
    or wanted.
I still want to travel,
    to experience the new,
but I also want to develop a home . . .
    a home
    of love and laughter,

a home
>   where things begin
>   and end. . . .
a home
>   filled with communication,
for our dreams can continue to grow
>   if we remember
to take time
>   to love
and understand each other
>   and our ever-changing life.
The snow continues
>   to fall outside . . .
I find warmth
>   in our home
for we are here together,
>   just us.

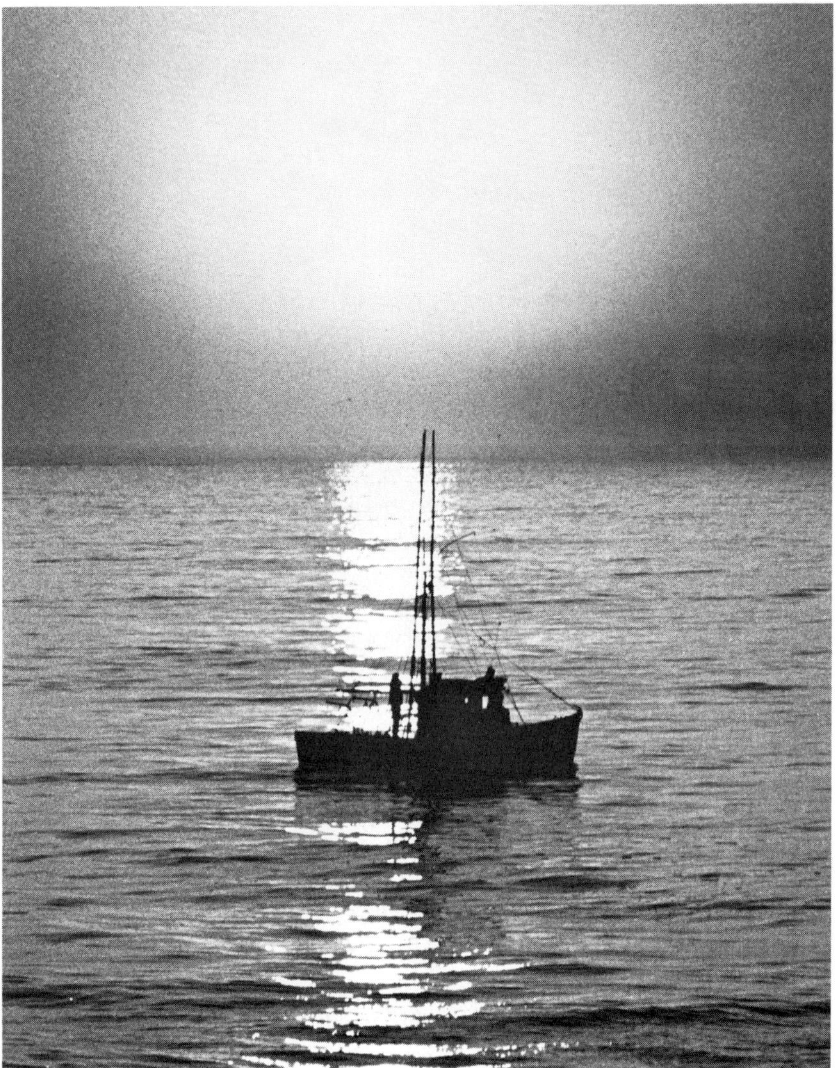

There are a few hours of the day
that are mine,
    when the work is done,
        the hectic pace is over
  and the lights of the city
      have provided a radiant glow.
It's time for me to relax, to enjoy,
    to create,
        to experience.
    I smile silently
      for I have
          nothing to accomplish . . .
I have the time
    to enjoy . . .
the time to just be.

I'm watching from afar,
and I'm concerned . . .
      you're struggling,
alone,
      withdrawing,
           sharing nothing but
the signs of your internal struggle.

Criticism has covered
your usual feelings of acceptance
          and I am afraid . . .

Afraid to venture in,
      to ask what is wrong
or to share where I am.

I'm concerned . . .
      you're struggling . . .
Your face is tight,
      your manner confused,
but your strength cannot be denied.

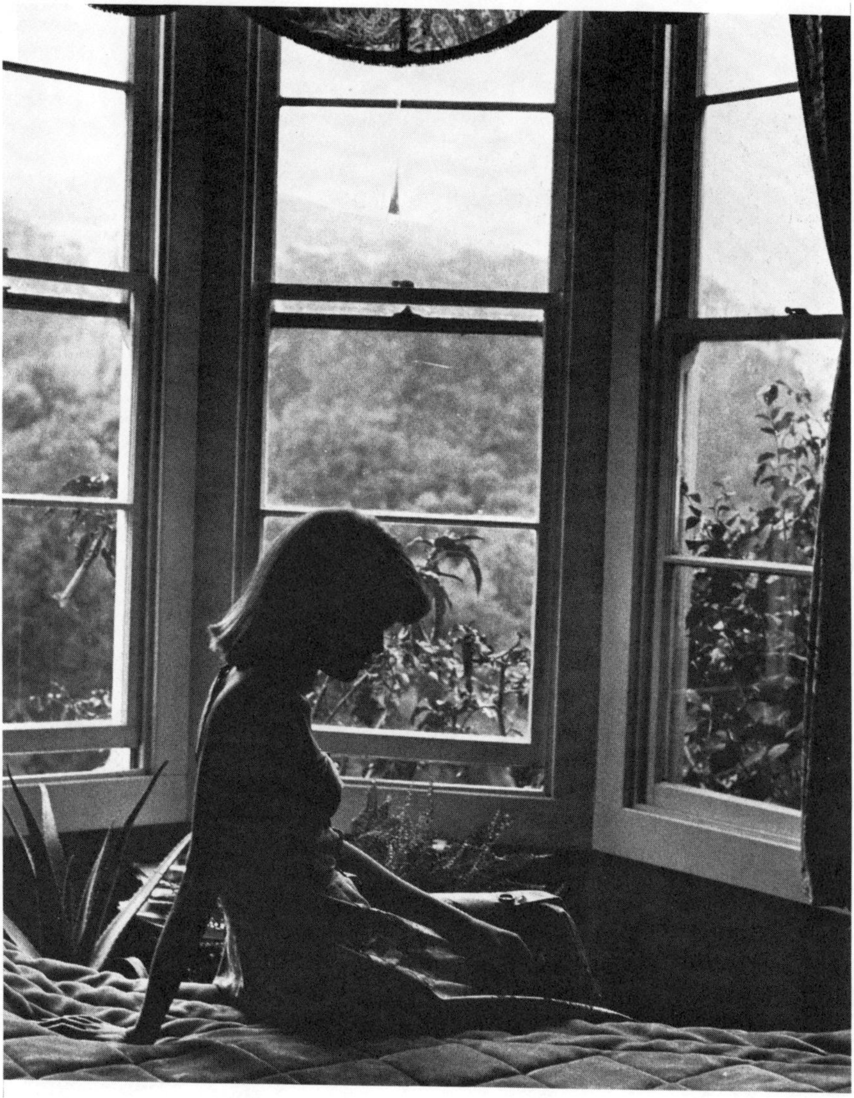

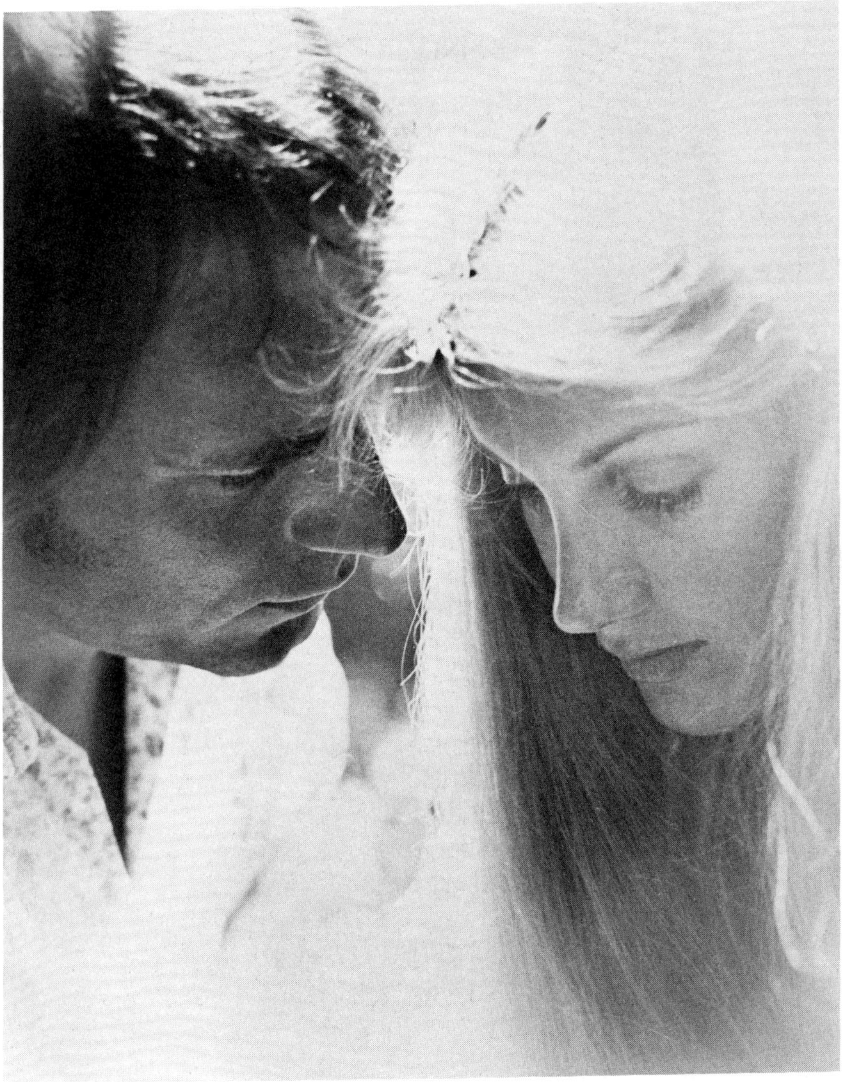

She talked to him for hours,
sharing her hurts and expressing
her doubts.
Months had passed
since they had parted
and now it was time
to resolve their conflicts,
to end the cancer of anxiety
which had lived within her
for so long.
He spoke of his life,
where he had been
and how he felt now.
She traveled back to a conversation
which had happened over a year ago.
She had heard the whole thing before.
All this time, and nothing had changed.
He felt the same,
unable to make a decision,
wanting to, but unable to venture in.
The frustration and hurt returned . . .
At times people find each other,
but at other times . . .

They parted . . . nothing had changed.
Her tears slowly prepared her for sleep.

I'm vulnerable right now . . .
    alone
        and lonely,
out of control,
    insecure . . .
    but not sure why.
My life is becoming a blur . . .
Motion,
      too much motion,
    tension,
      too much tension,
    no closure . . . conflicts . . .
        overwhelmed . . .
I'm vulnerable right now . . .
Please be gentle . . .

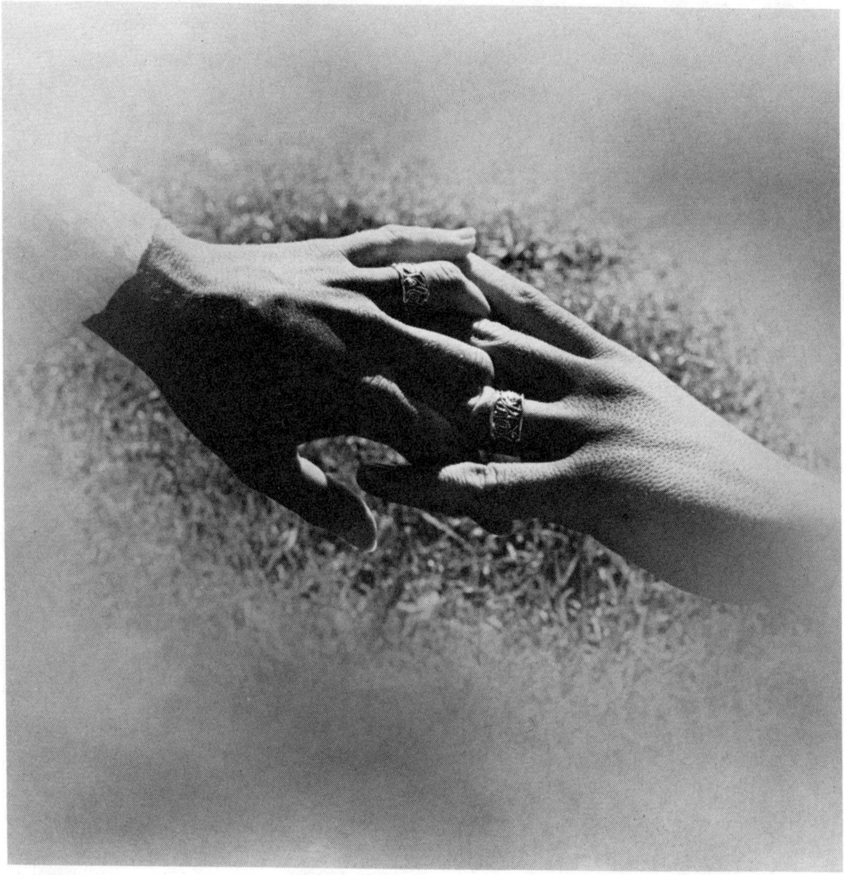

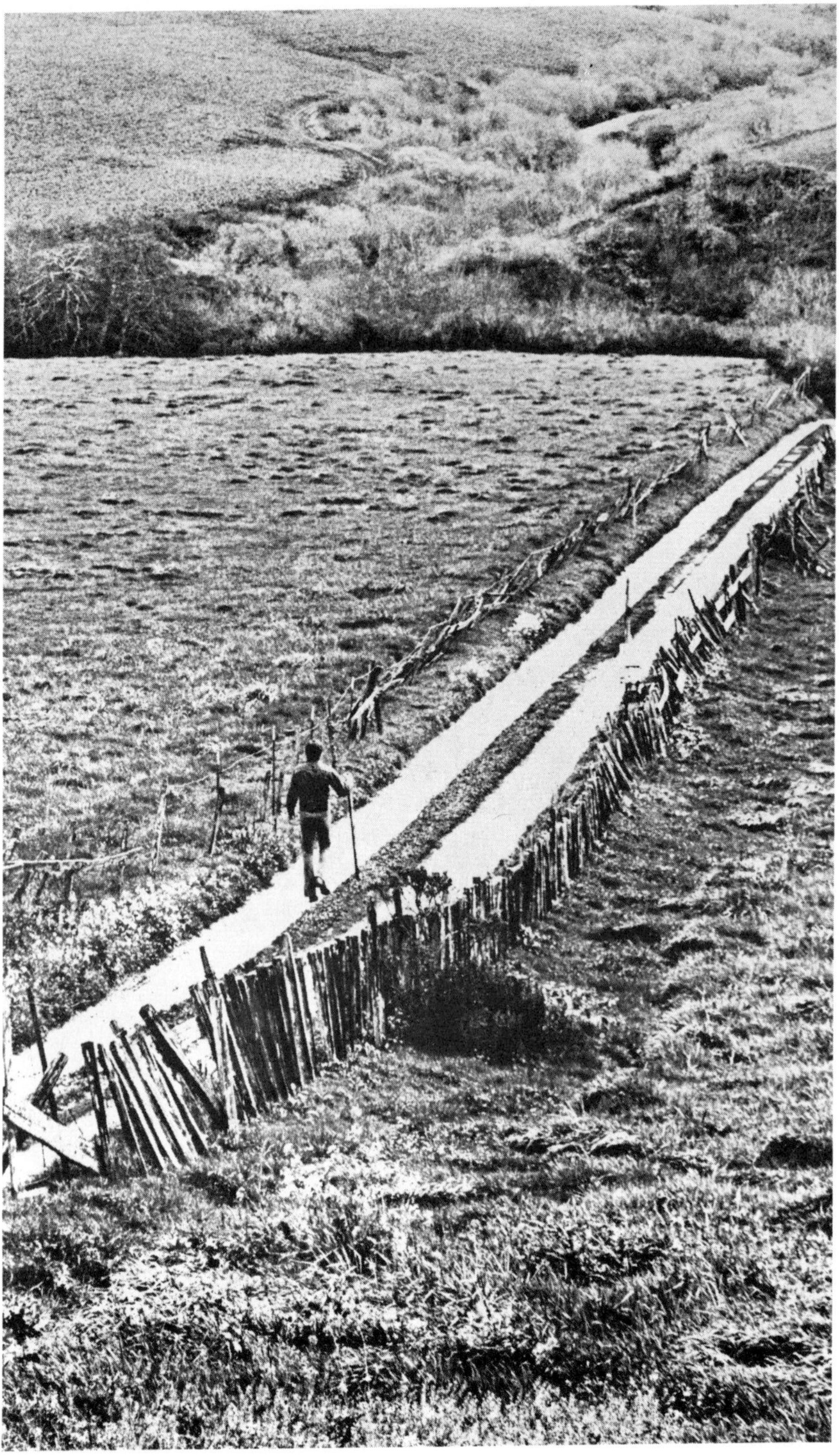

Where does my security come from?
     you?
          me?
               others?
And where does it go?

My path continues,
     my journey will be long,
          but where it will end,
I do not know.

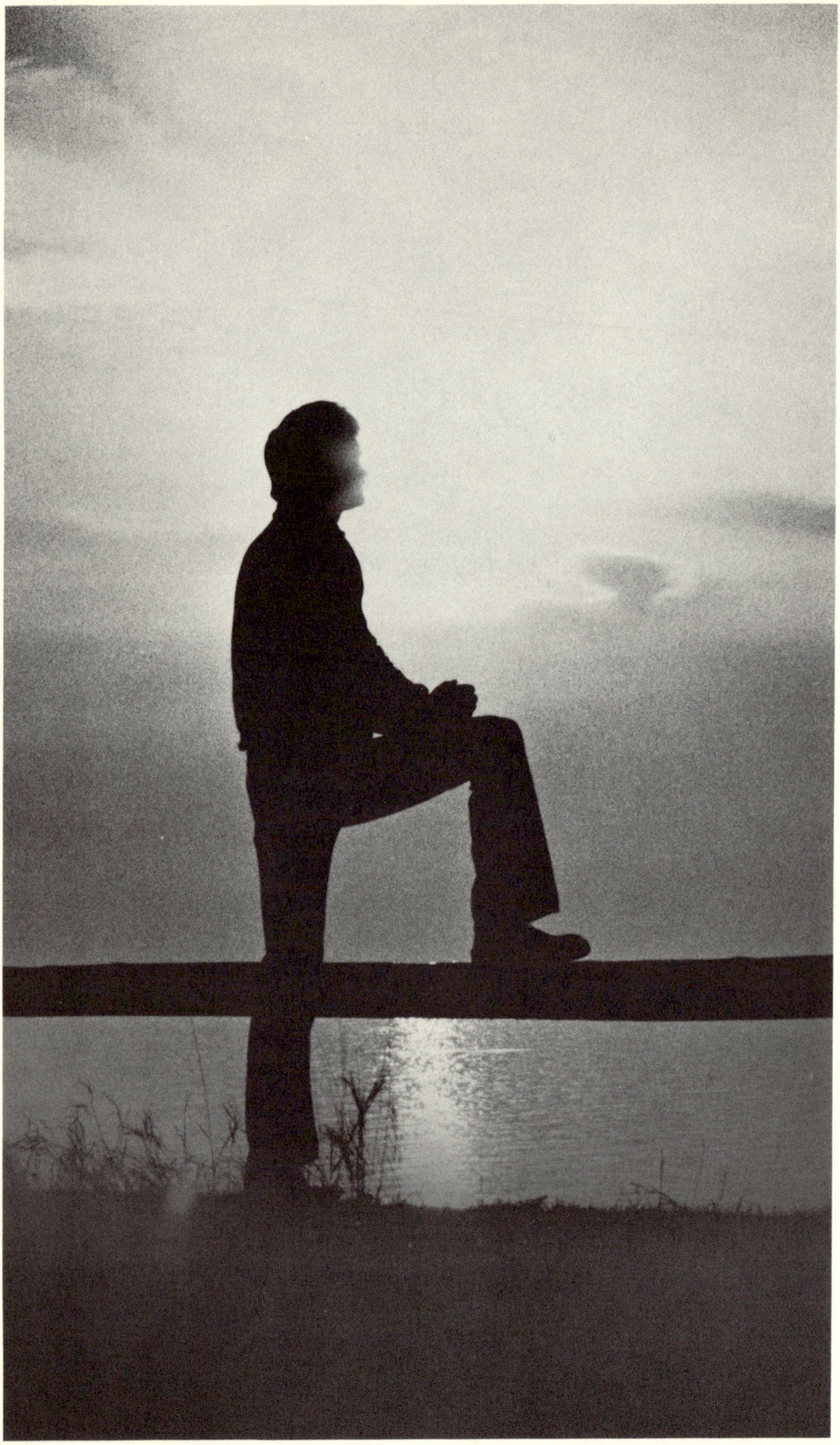

Sometimes late at night,
hours after I have gone to sleep
I awake abruptly,
my mind moving strongly,
searching wildly for something,
        something . . .
but I do not know what.

I travel back to the past
to re-discover truths that have escaped me
and memories which
        were once so fresh.
I think about myself
        and the changes I have made.

I'm no longer the person
I was yesterday.
I have grown,
        changed
and am happy to be
        who I am now,
contented with where I am.
But then I remember
        something
I learned so long ago.
"For everything you gain,
        you might also lose something."
And I am sad
for I am not aware
of what I might have lost,
        only aware of what I have gained.
And for moments I want to go back
        and re-experience,
                re-discover
        something
I might have missed . . .

We were young then
and life was an adventure,
    filled with excitement . . .

We lived each day
to the fullest
and no matter how
    hard times were,
  no matter what
    the pressures were,
we knew things
    would change . . .
Happiness was what we strived for.
We were young then . . .
We always had tomorrow . . .

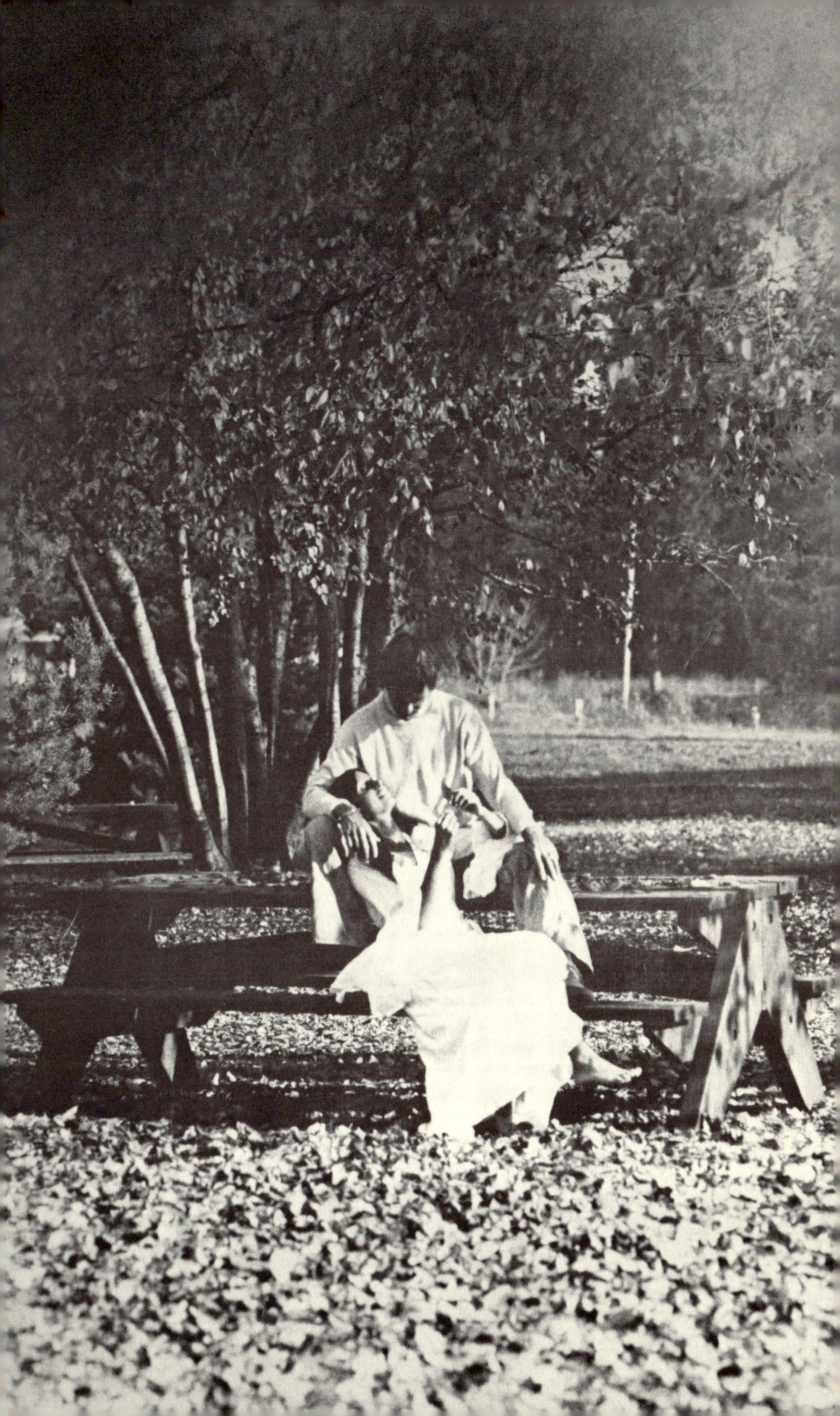

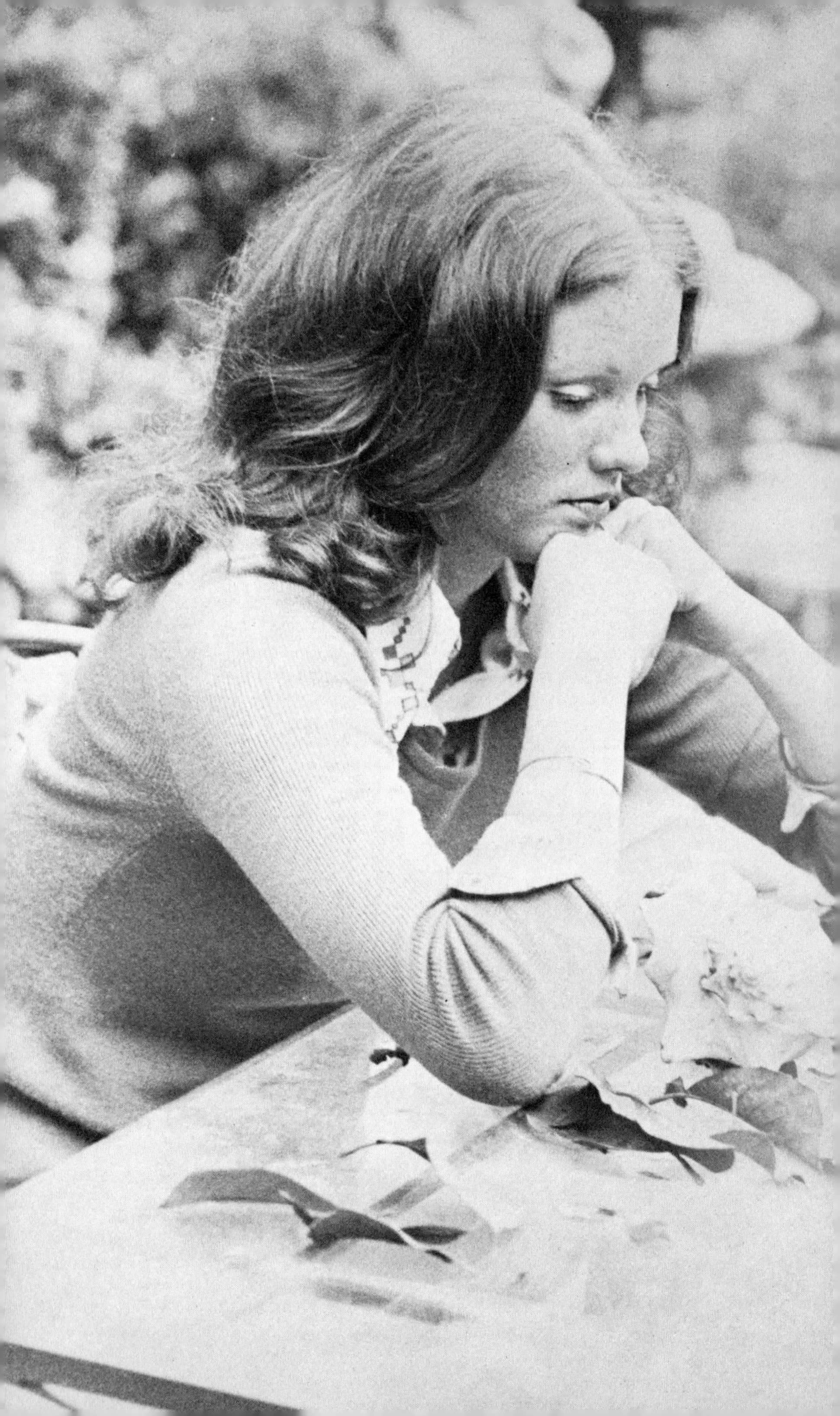

What now?
We've talked for hours
but nothing has been said.

We care so deeply
but our feelings are lost
when we desperately try
to find each other.

You avoid my glances.
I talk about nothing . . .
Silence . . .
Finally the waiter announces
that it's time to close.

For moments our eyes meet
and I'm somewhat refreshed,
because even though it's painful
we'll try again.

Love is so hard to understand,
at times.

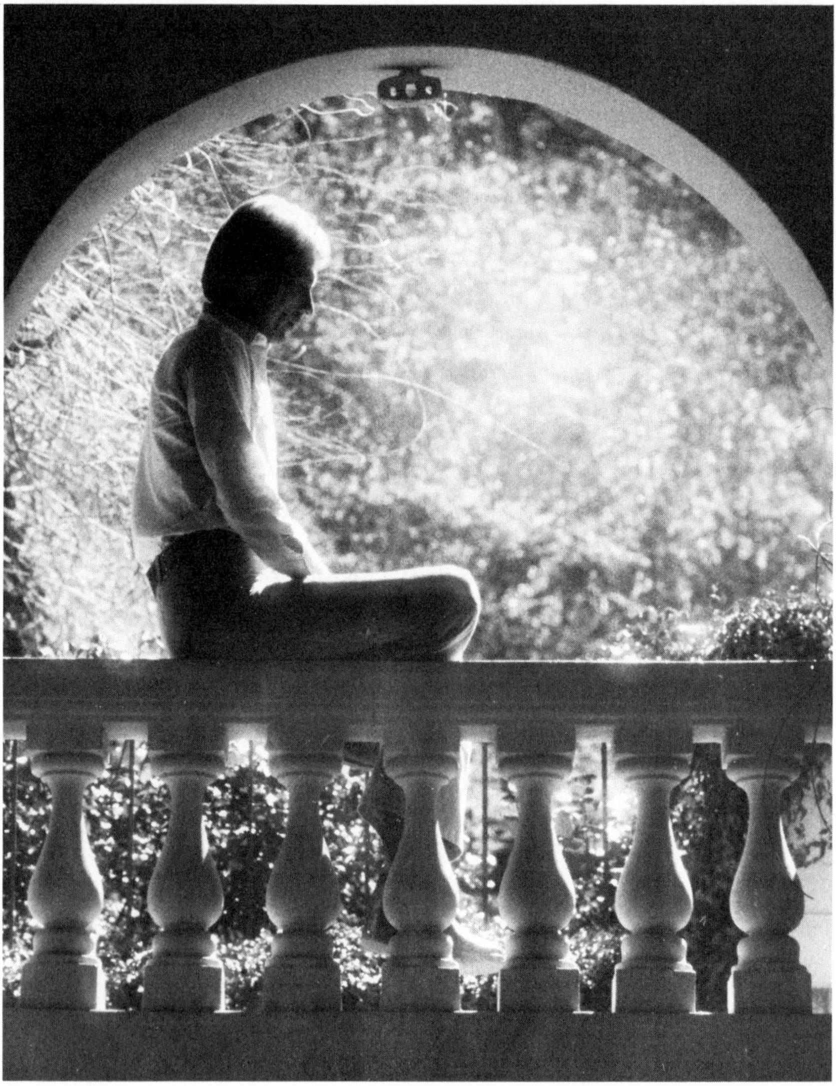

Again,
it returns . . .
a feeling inside . . .
the yearning to travel,
    to move around,
        to find whatever there is.

I have a thirst in me
which will never
        be fully satisfied.
It is the desire to go beyond,
    to know tomorrow,
        to explore . . .

I want to explore me,
    my many emotions and feelings.
I want to explore you
    so I can begin to understand.
I want to explore more of my world,
    for it beholds my dreams,
        even my "impossible dream . . ."

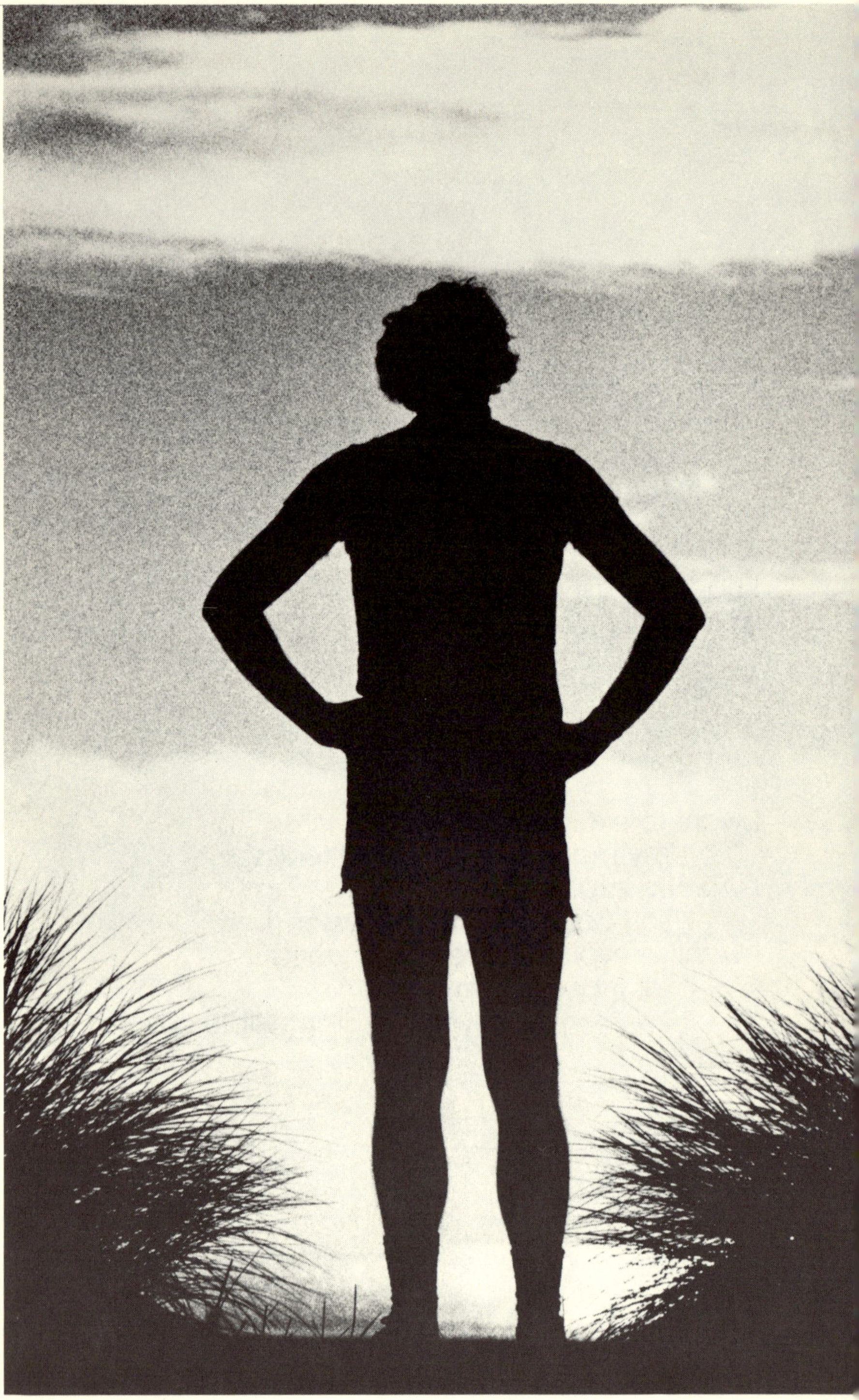

I wonder...
    do all people want
        to "better" themselves?
    do all people seek
        answers about life?
    do all people experience
        many emotions and feelings
            each day?
    do all people have
        joys and sorrows,
            ups and downs?
    do all people have
        regrets and satisfactions?
    do all people want
        to love and be loved?
    do all people realize
        that today is
            the most important time
            of their lives?
    do all people...
        I wonder...

I'm upset with you,
really upset with you,
because we cannot talk.

I play a game,
trying to be nice
but inside,
    I'm being
        so damned phony.

I want to be friends . . .
to be open and honest
    with each other
but I find us
    caught
        in a pattern . . .
A pattern where we
        deny reality
and act as if everything
    is just fine.
And then we part,
and I scream
from being so tense,
        so upset,
and I hate it . . .
and I think you
        feel the same
but I'm not sure . . .

I haven't taken the risk
        to ask you . . .

Are you as miserable
            as I am?
Are you upset with me?
Do I understand
            how you feel
or am I only guessing?

My God! This hurts . . .
How much more
            will I take
until I take the risk
      to talk to you
about what I'm feeling
                  inside?

I know it's a risk
            to be honest,
but if I don't,
            slowly,
      I believe
            both of us
will be destroyed,
            separately,
while we continue
            to be nice
                  on the outside . . .

Life is never the same.
At times I find myself on the brink
    of defeat,
        close to drowning . . .
and I cry out for help,
but I know the answers must come from
        within.
I need your help
    but I must help myself . . .
I must get beyond
    where I am today.
I must change,
    I must grow . . .
I begin to gain confidence, security,
        faith in myself.
Struggling, I reach a plateau
    and I feel better about myself
        and my world.
I become comfortable.
But later I am bored
    or threatened
        or unhappy with myself . . .
And the process begins
    once again . . .
        conflict
            struggle
        decisions
            action
        closure and fulfillment.

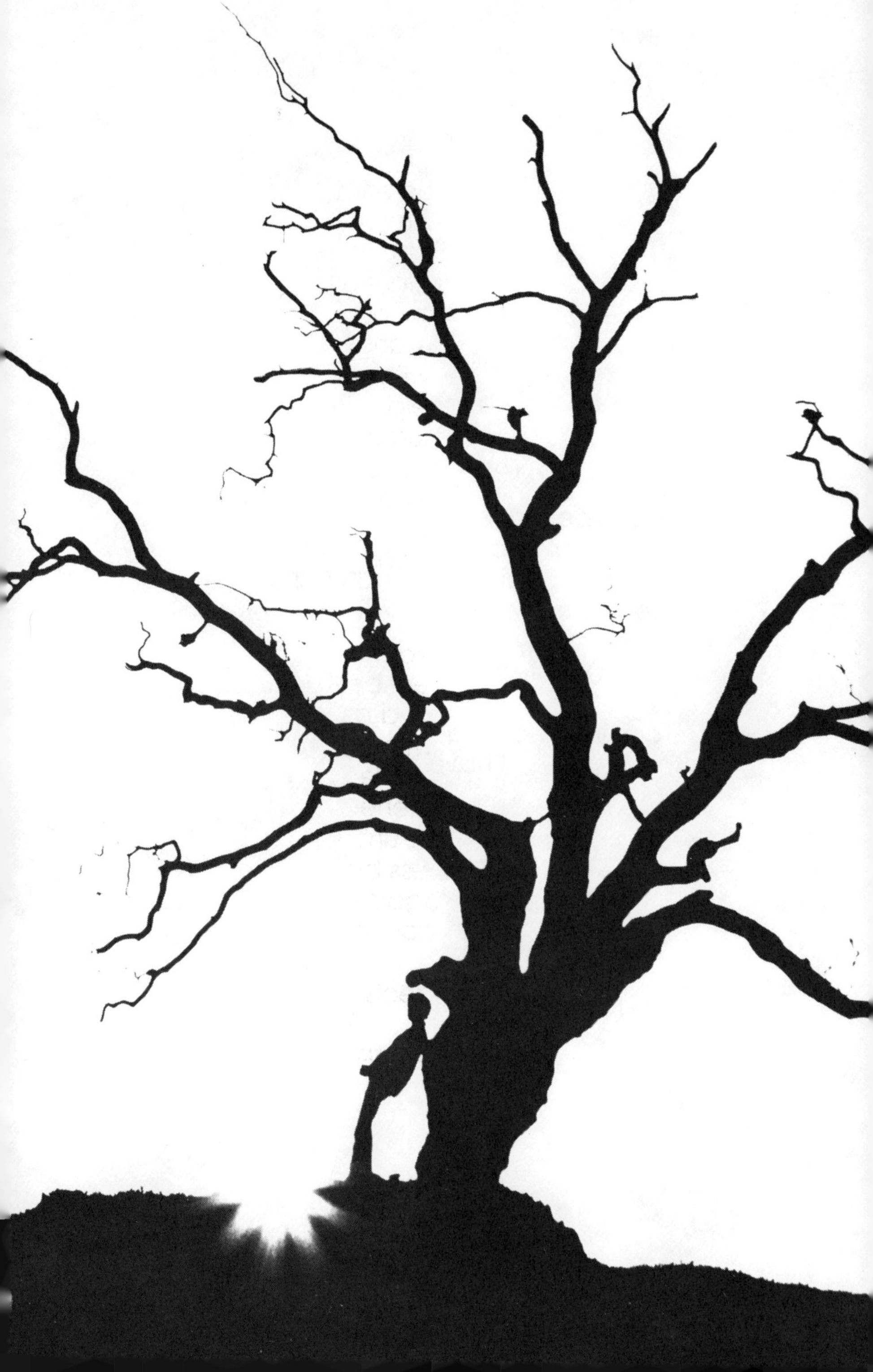

The experience is over for now
      but I have learned . . .
           I know it can happen . . .
I reach out for tomorrow,
    ready,
    excited,
        open . . .
Today has changed my life.
        I have grown . . .

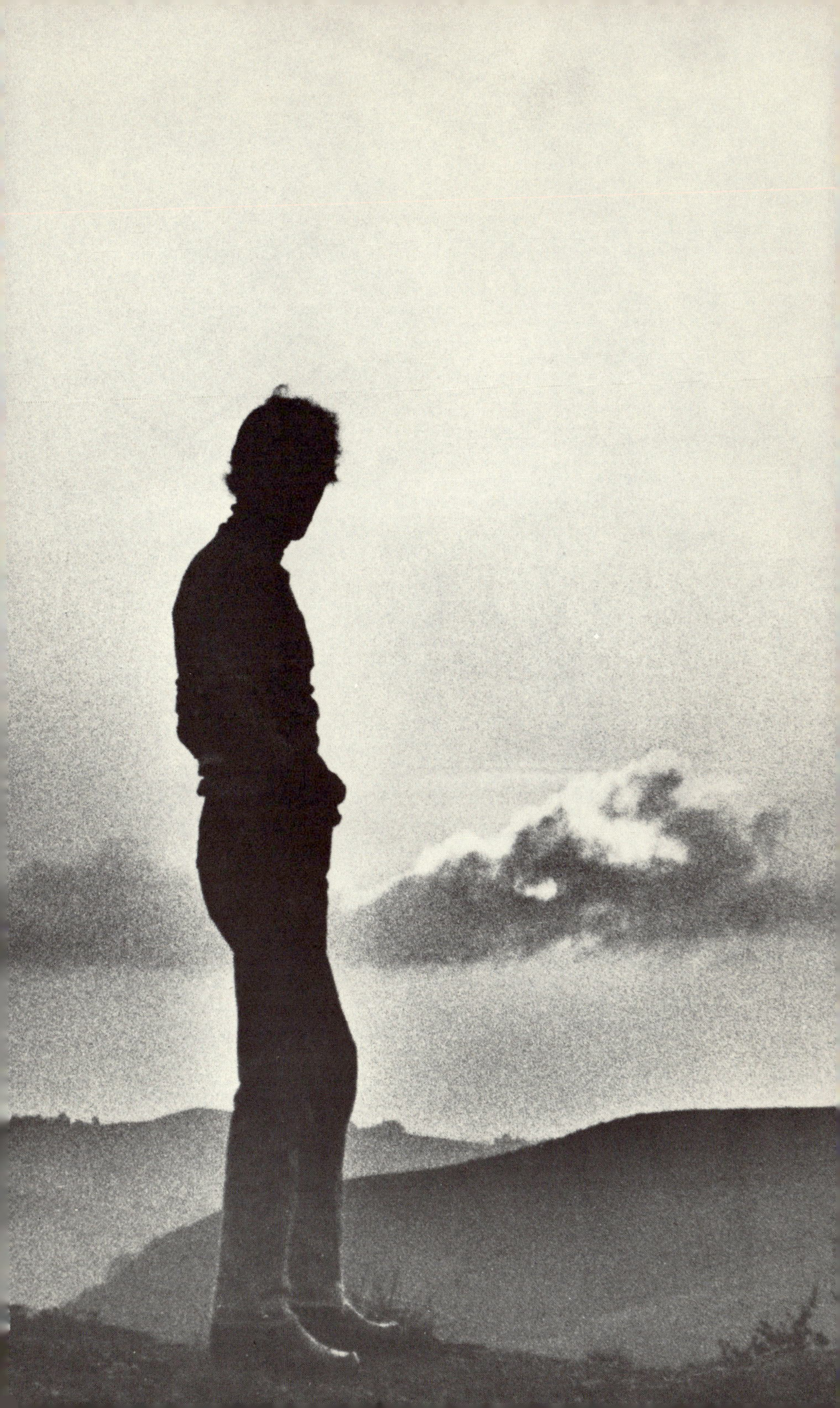

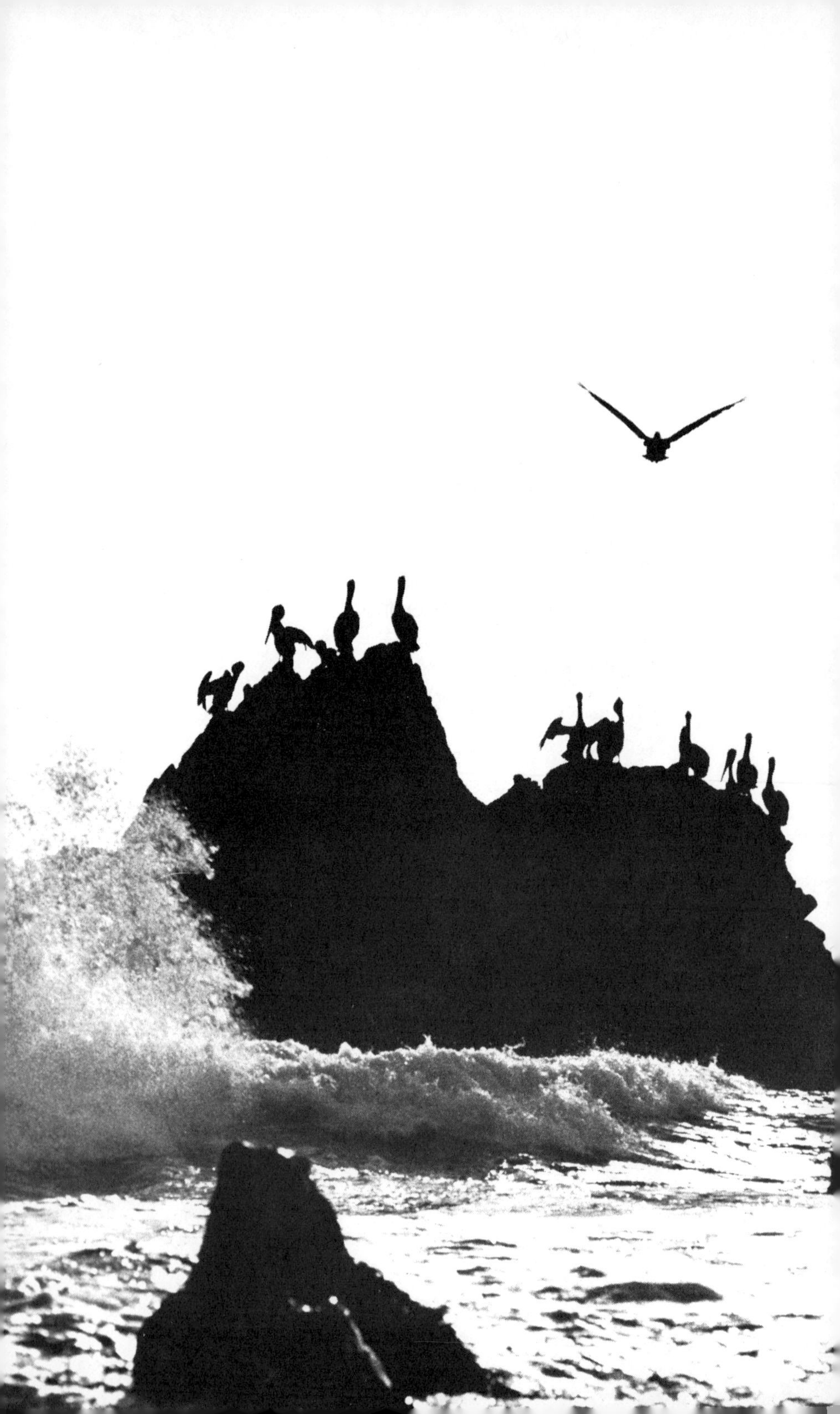

I can feel it!
I'm breaking out!
The Mad Hatter has lost!
I'm beginning to unwind,
        to slow down.
Once again I'm relearning
        a painful lesson.
I cannot save the world
        by charging straight ahead . . .

My world begins with me
and I must take time . . .

Without meeting my own needs
I am of less value
        to everyone,
               including myself.

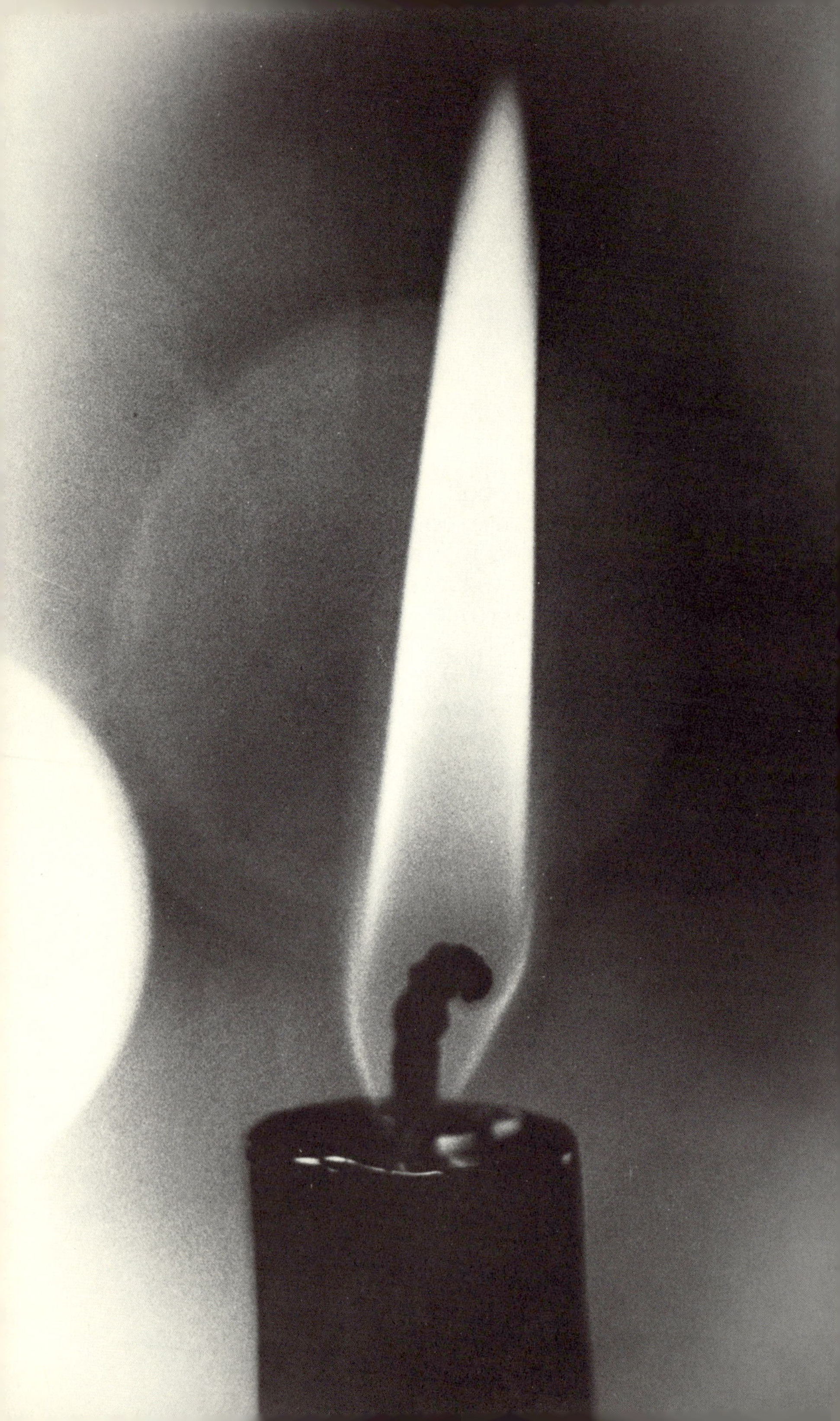

Sunday night,
        no demands.
The paper has been read,
        the football games are over,
and we are alone . . .
Soft music fills the room,
        candlelight adds
    to our feelings.
We have slowed down,
        finally . . .
      a glass of wine,
    a simple dinner,
tenderness
      and time to share love.
With the dawn we will begin once again
      but tonight belongs to us.
Our wine glasses touch,
      our eyes meet,
and in our hearts we know
      that the world is ours.

There is a child within me,
the one who has always been inside,
    the one who will always remain.

It is the child within me
which allows me to laugh
        and smile,
    to run and play,
  to create,
    to love . . .
My child provides
    my highest emotions and feelings . . .
My child offers me visions
  and dreams.
This child is the gateway
    of my passions.

I am an adult now,
    with adult ways and habits.
Childhood left me many years ago,
    replaced by a more complex
      way of life.
But I am not sad.
The child remains,
    forever . . .

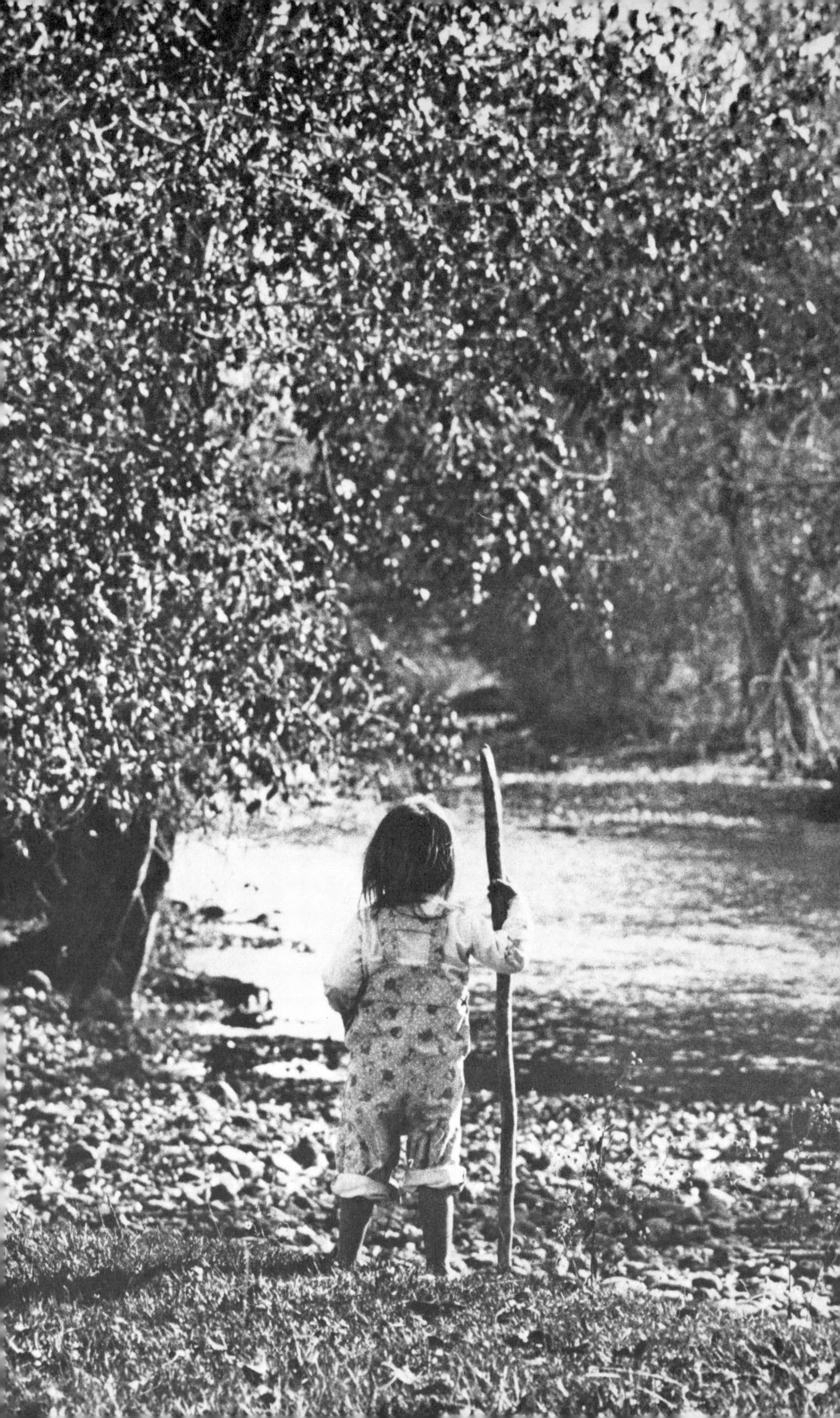

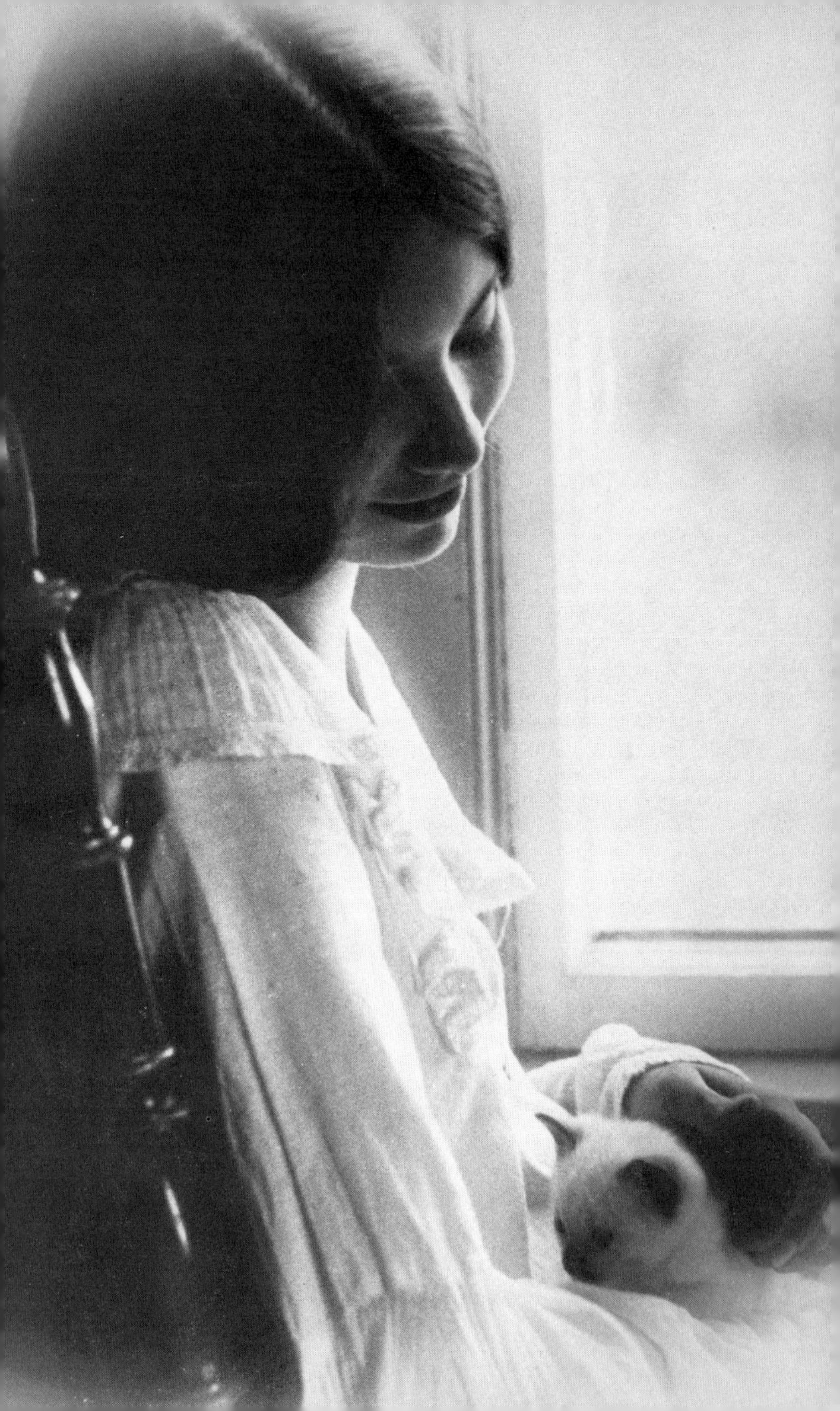

Yesterday was filled
with sunshine and happiness,
but on the news last night
the weatherman informed us
    of possible changes.

As I write this,
    after a good night's sleep,
I sit in morning solitude
    and listen . . .
        to nothing in particular,
           just the sounds of morning.

I have been so busy
the past few days . . .
    and now . . .
        morning,
           rainy weather
and time for reflection.
I am very contented,
    just living my morning
        solitude.

We've been in the mountains
    for several days now.
People and the city
    seem so far away.
We're learning to slow down,
    to take time,
    to think of our own needs . . .

You have a look of contentment
    on your face,
    a look I don't see too often
        in the city.

After dinner tonight,
    we'll build a fire,
        read a few pages
    and settle into love,
    where moments are hours
        and everything is forever.
As the fire slowly dies out
we'll drift to sleep
    safe and secure within
        each other's arms . . .

Goodnight my love.
We kiss
        and gently
      prepare for sleep
knowing that
     we are together . . .
The fire is
     slowly burning out . . .
Your eyes are closed now.
I stare at you
     trying to capture
         the look on your face,
    a look of contentment
      and love,
    the look that shows me
        you are secure . . .
Your body relaxes,
    a small smile appears . . .
You breathe deeply,
     asleep now.
I hold you gently in my arms,
      trying to capture
        forever
     the feelings I have
        for you.
I am content . . .
      sleep is mine . . .

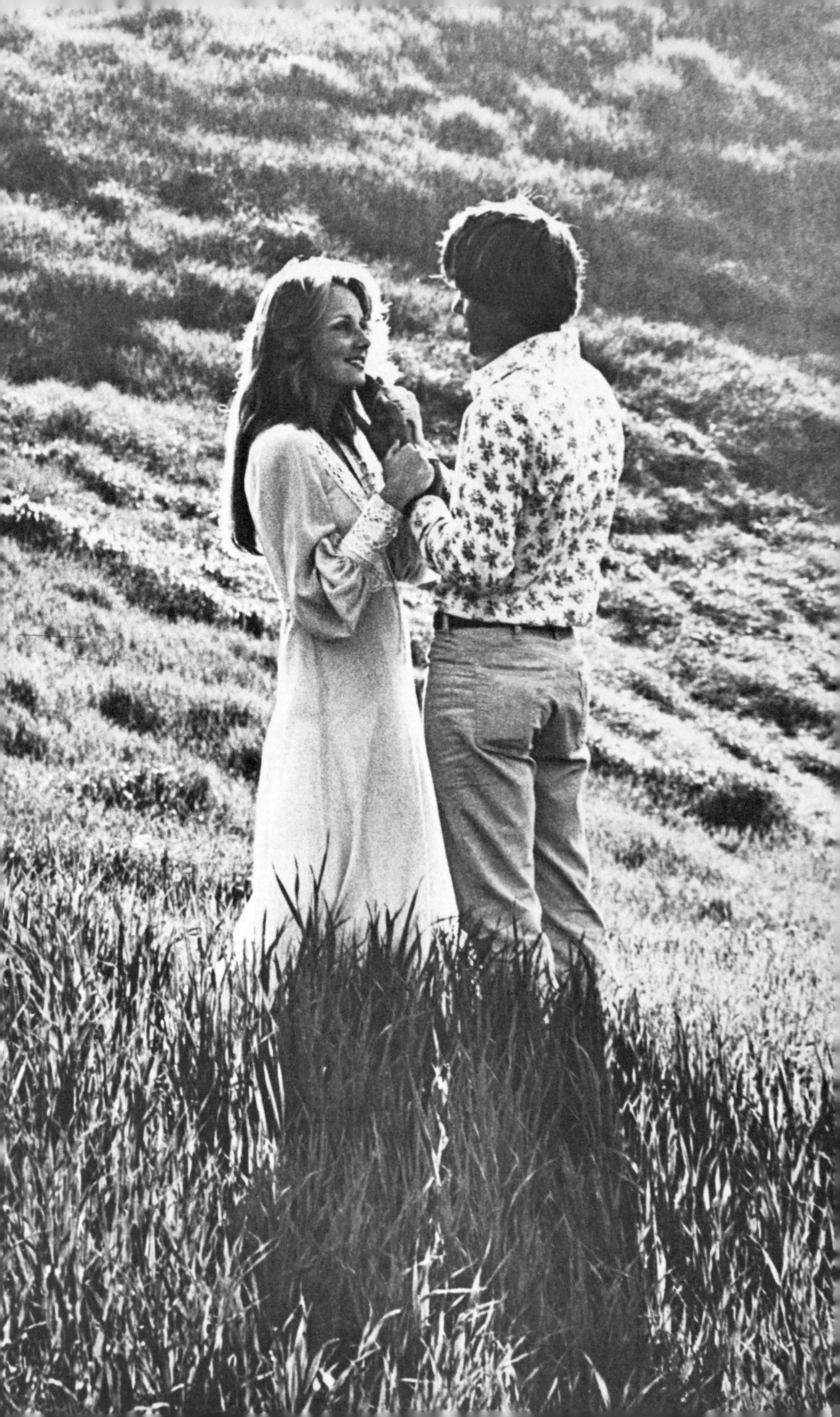

You're special for you are
one of the only people
who gives me honest,
    direct feedback.
Most people either
    don't know how
        or find it too big
      a risk
but you're different.

Your sensitivity,
    awareness
and honest feedback help me
to continue
to grow and change.
How lucky I am
to have you as my friend.

You strive for perfection,
    to be everything
        you can possibly be.
And most of the time
        you succeed
    but there are other times
      when you fall short,
    when you are unsure of yourself,
        not totally in control of your emotions.
You slip back a step
but . . .
        with tomorrow . . .

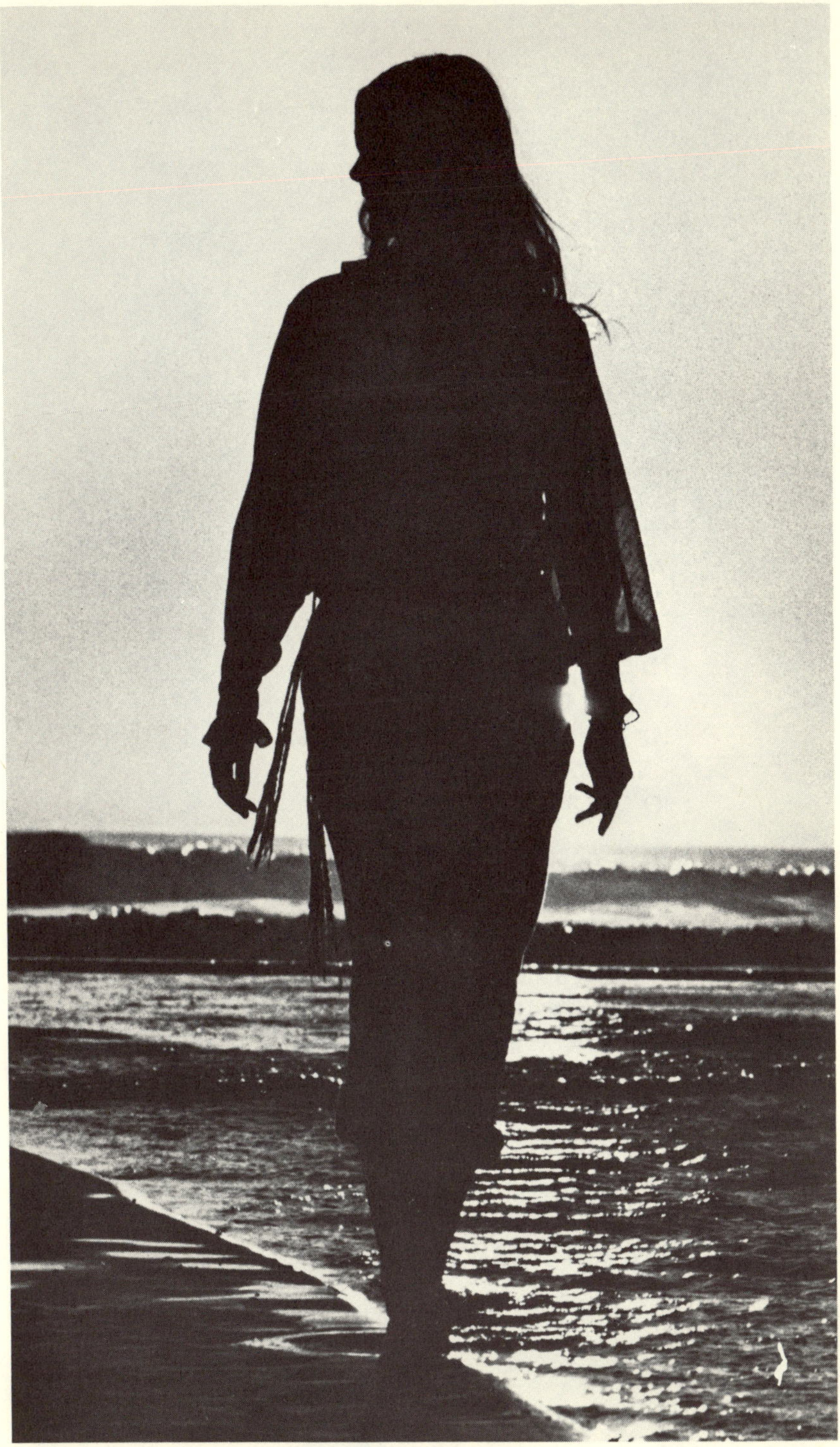

We had a conflict tonight,
a tough one that took
several hours to resolve.
We stayed with it,
realizing how good
we would feel
when we came to closure
and discovered answers
to our problem.
I want to thank you
for believing in the process,
for caring enough
to deal with the pain
      and anguish,
and for realizing, once again,
that conflict can lead
      to growth.
Now we have parted
and I feel good,
for I know that we are both loved.

We began with hesitation,
not knowing what lay ahead.
Carefully, inching along,
slipping at times,
taking risks at others,
we continued,
but the farther we traveled
the more difficult it became.
Finally, we neared the top . . .

We climbed a mountain today
although we never left the room.
Our conflict was over,
we had learned to communicate.
The summit was ours . . .

How can I have been so blind?
Through my fantasies I had developed
the idea of what I wanted in another person.
I dreamed of tenderness
        and the time to experience.
I had created the "ideal" person for me.
Someone I didn't know,
        but someone who could exist.
                I had my dreams . . .
And then I left for awhile.
I had new experiences,
        met different people,
became involved in a new world.
I was searching . . .
                I had time to think, to reflect.
Slowly I began to see my dream
                and to understand what I was
                          searching for.
How could I have been so blind?
                My dream world does exist . . .
at home,
        with you my love.

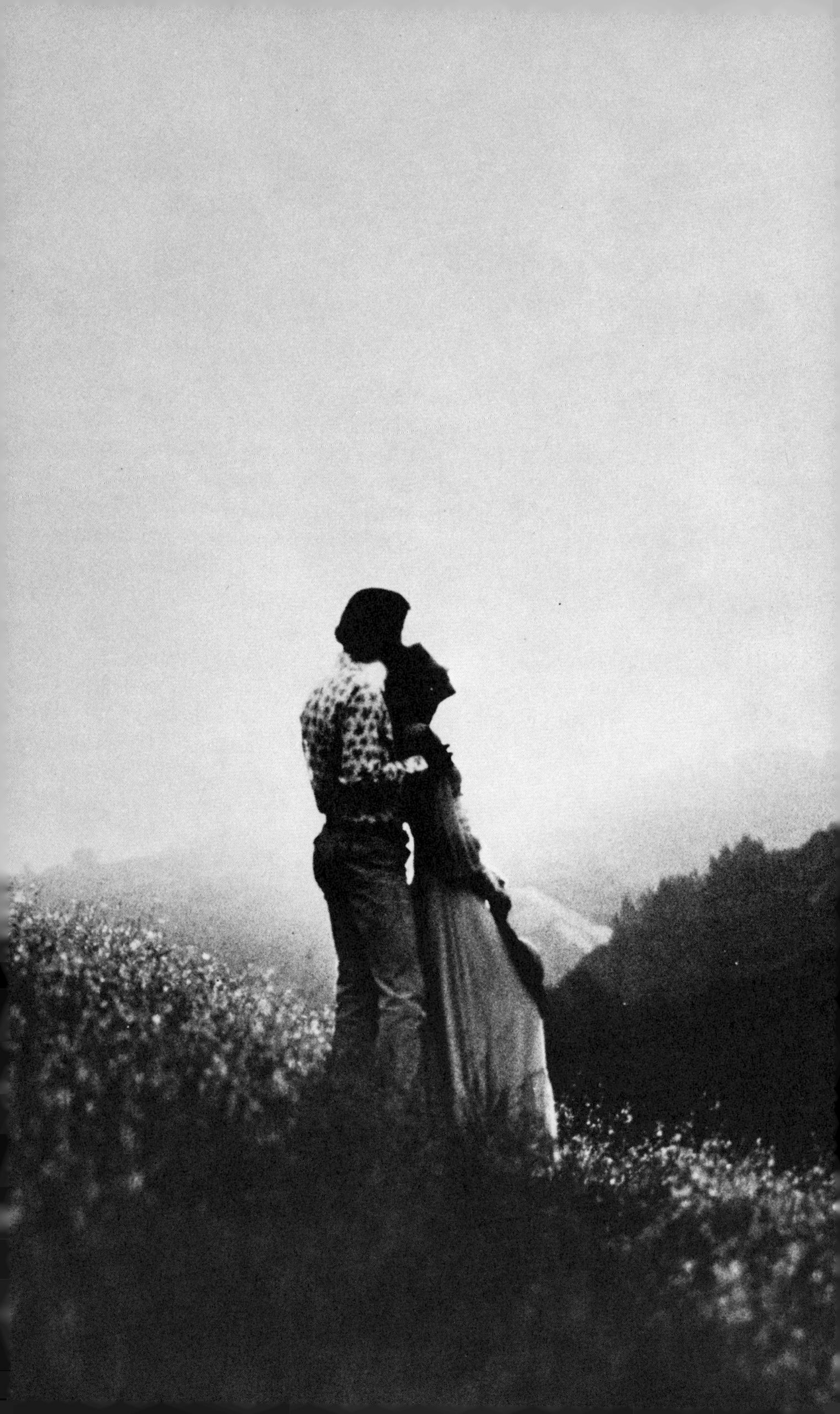

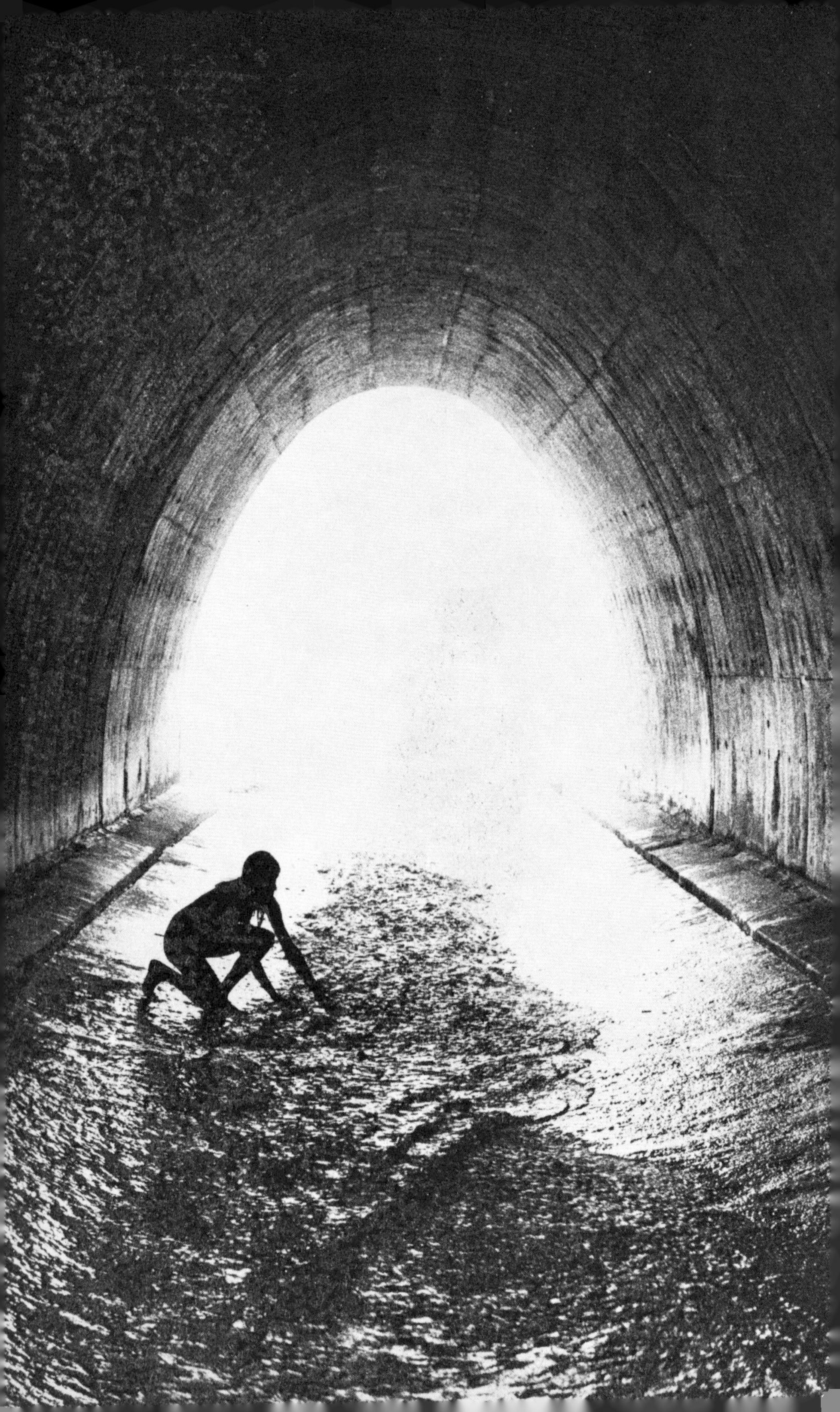

Sometimes I get depressed
        when I think of all
                the millions of people
           who have lived with me
                or before me.
I think of the vastness
of the entire universe
        and I see myself as
such a small speck.
And I realize that
        almost every idea
           has already been discovered
     and that all feelings
          have been experienced.
I become overwhelmed . . .
But then I realize that I am important,
        that there never has been,
     nor will there ever be
          another person
    exactly like me.
I am unique,
     one of a kind.
My thoughts and ideas are refreshing
for they lead me to my own understanding.
My feelings are my own . . .
My life is my opportunity
     to combine everything.
There are millions of others in the world . . .
       and just like everyone else, I am unique.

Many times I write about others
but today I am writing
        about me
I'm attempting to understand me.
and the experiences
                I have had.
What a luxury —
     to have time just for me.

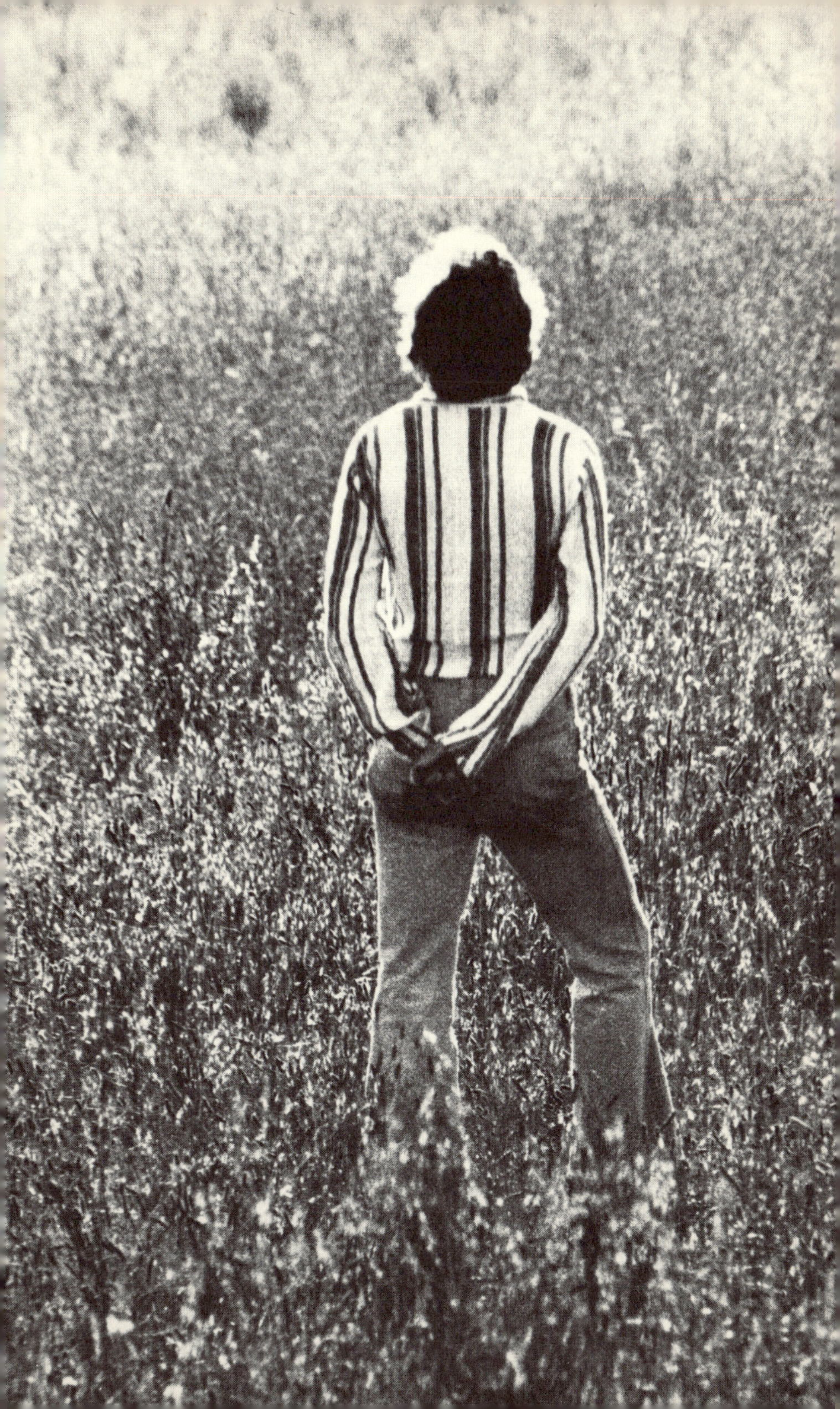

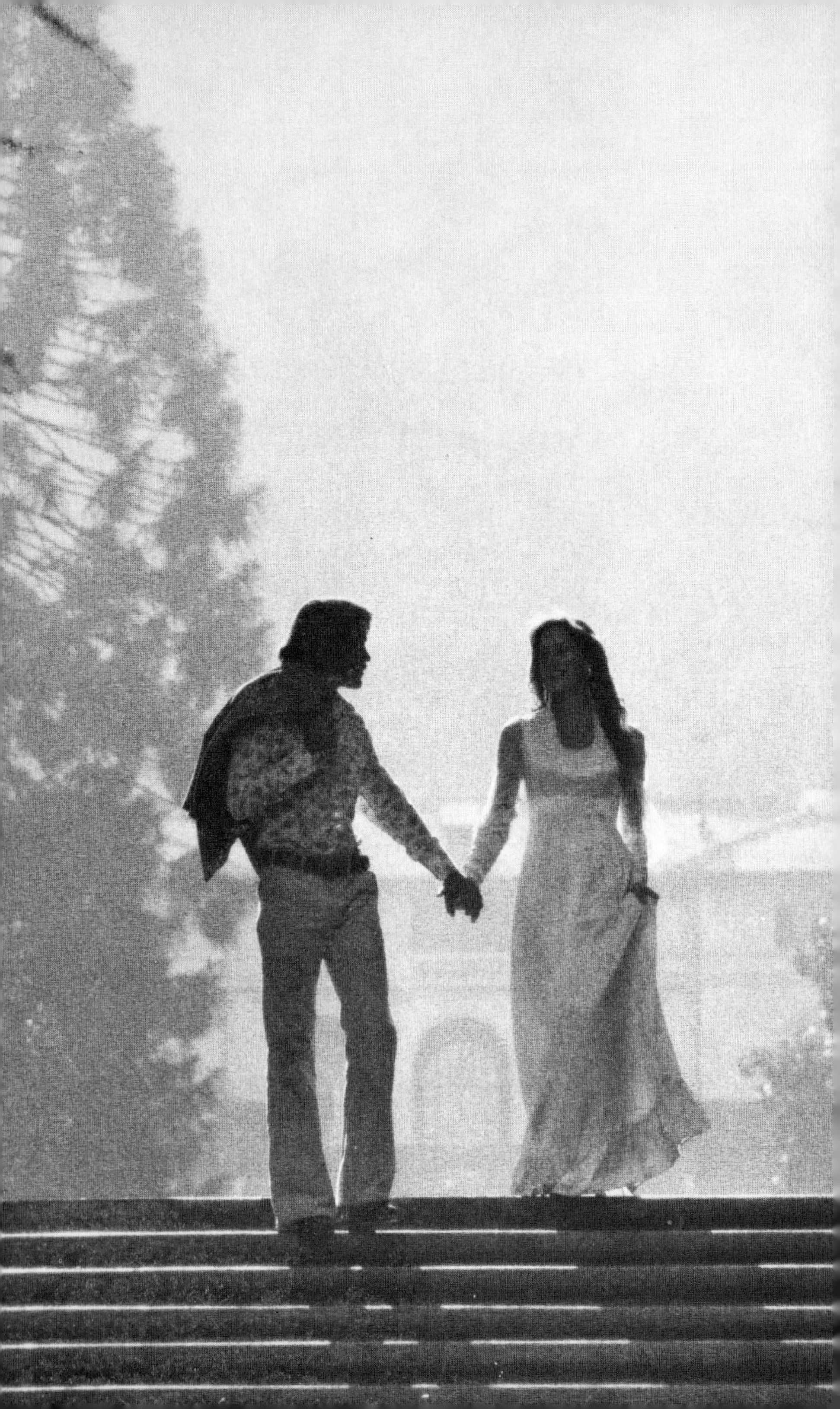

Out of a crowd
I began to notice you.
I think it was
the gentle look
on your face.

You sat silently,
not looking outward,
but feeling inward,
while your mind
was wandering,
exploring your world . . .

You caught my eye,
And I continued
to watch you.

I have touched your hand
and shared your glance.
We have communicated
through our moods
and through our words.
Our hearts are warm . . .

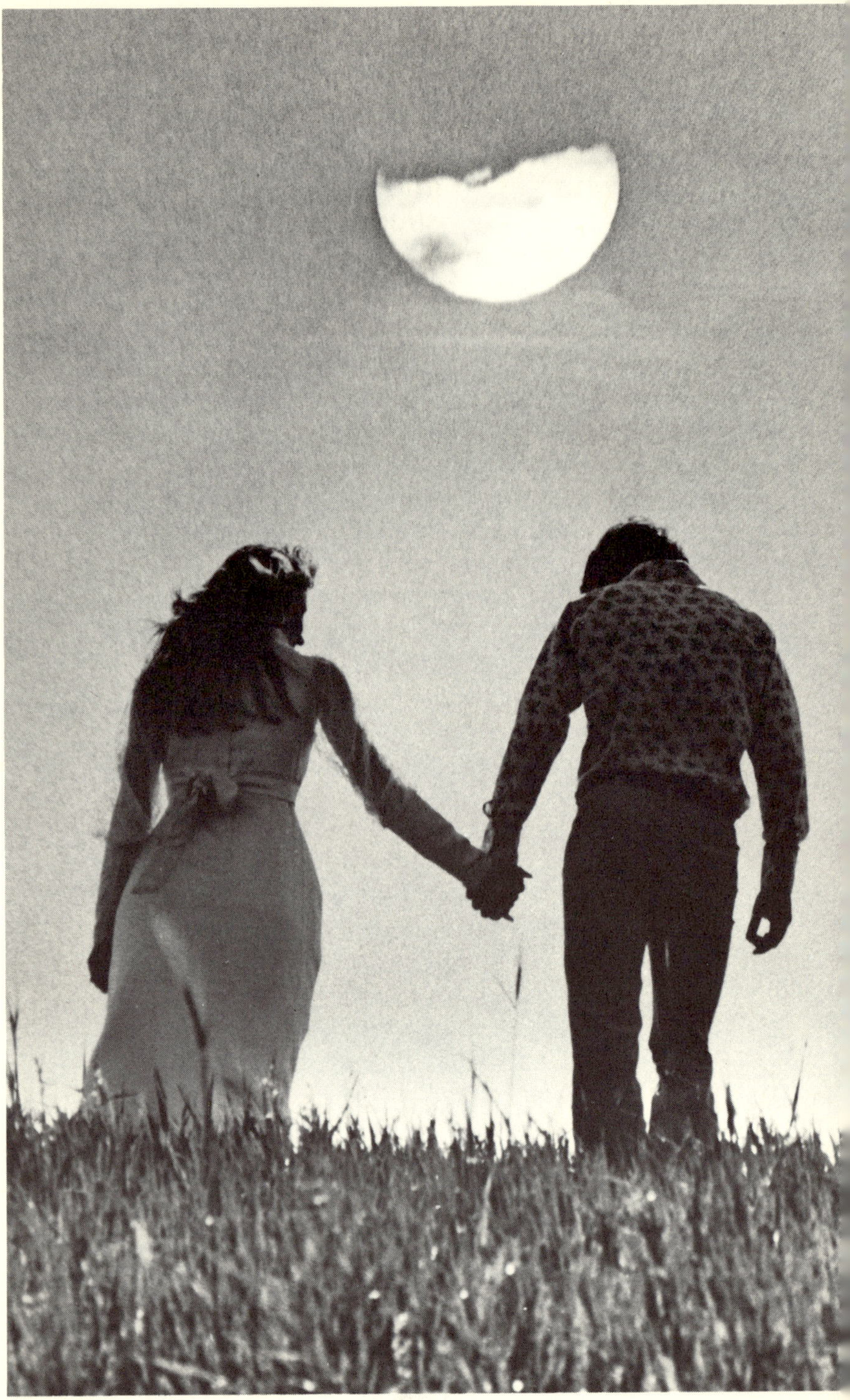

When I'm feeling down,
    when I find myself
        struggling,
    searching,
I know I can always think of you
    and realize
        that you accept
    and love me,
that you will help me
    through the night.
Through your comfort
    and questioning
    you help me face
        the darkness of conflict
and strive for the joys of sunshine.

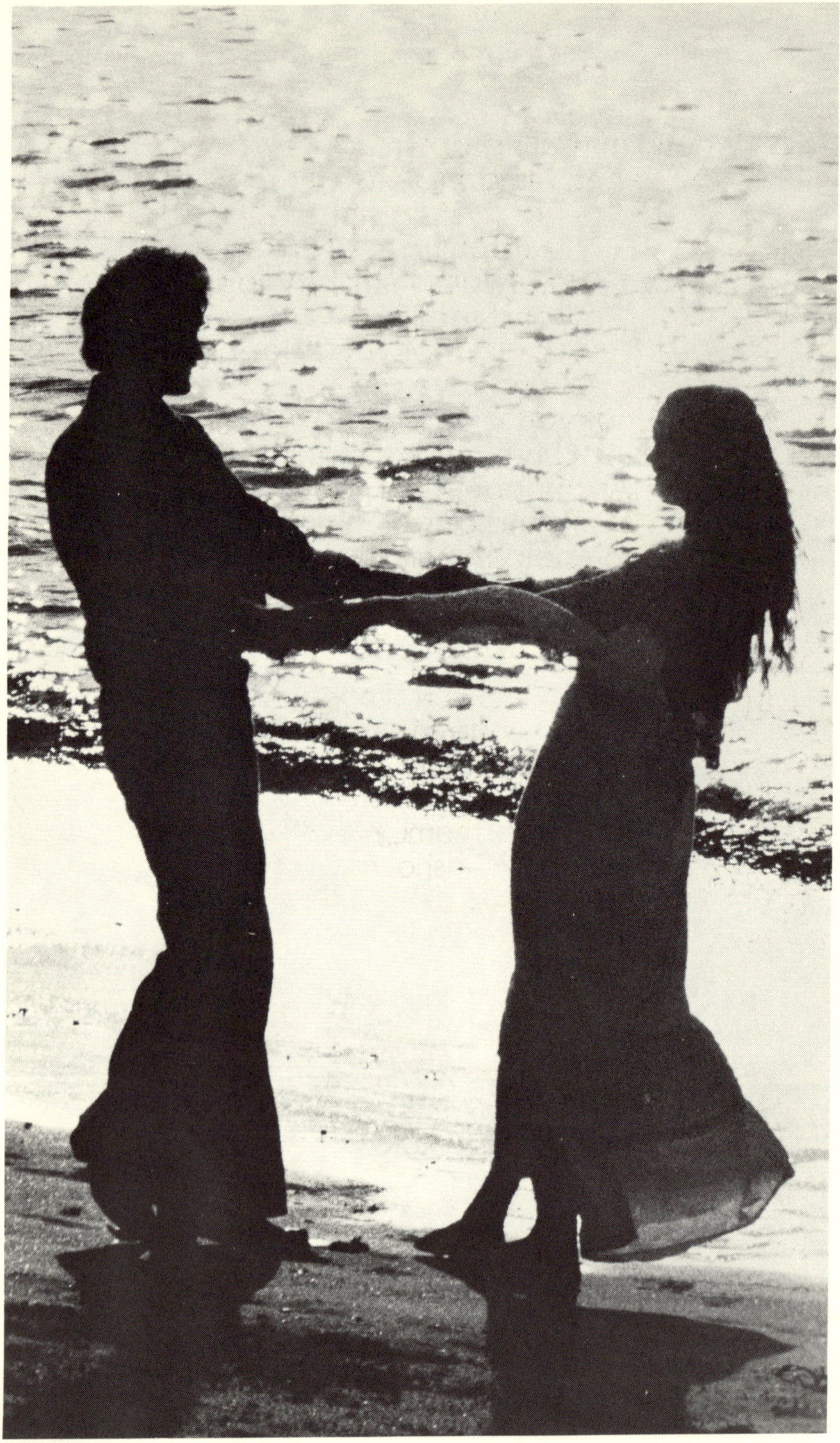

Les,

And now we begin
to say good-bye,
for we must part
and go our separate
ways . . .
But we leave
      so much stronger . . .
We have given each other
something that will strengthen
us on our journeys,
      the memories of
          sharing,
              respect,
                and love.

Love,
Joyce

BOOKS OF RELATED INTEREST

In GROWING TOGETHER, George and Donni Betts portray in words and photographs the crucial difference between merely falling in love and actually growing in love. 128 pages, soft cover, $4.95

George Betts says of his book, MY GIFT TO YOU: "My writing becomes a roadmap, not to show where I am going, but to let me relive where I have been. I share it with you in the hope that you can add another piece to this puzzle called life." 128 pages, soft cover, $4.95

In VISIONS OF YOU, George Betts uses poetry and photographs to express clearly and beautifully the yearnings and hopes and feelings we all have. His voice is that of a lover, a friend, a person who deeply cares. 128 pages, soft cover, $4.95

TEARS AND PEBBLES IN MY POCKETS by George Betts reveals conflict and struggle to be a vital part of growth, and invites us each to experience and develop. 96 pages, soft cover, $4.95

In the beautifully illustrated poem, SELF ESTEEM, world-renowned family therapist Virginia Satir presents an essential credo for the individual in modern society. 64 pages, soft cover, $3.95

In MAKING CONTACT, Virginia Satir discusses the essentials in interpersonal relationships and provides innovative techniques for improving communication with others. 96 pages, soft cover, $4.95

SPECTRUM OF LOVE by Walter Rinder is a sensitive prose-poem that expresses all of the power, honesty, and commitment of love. 64 pages, soft cover, $3.95

Available at your local book or department store or directly from the publisher. To order by mail, send check or money order to:

CELESTIAL ARTS
231 Adrian Road
Millbrae, California 94030

Please include $1.00 for postage and handling. California residents add 6% sales tax.